IL CANADÁ,
LE COLONIE INGLESI
Con
LA LUIGIANA E FLORIDA
di nuova Projezione

VENEZIA 1800.
Presso Antonio Zatta

Kansas . . . the 34th Star

Kansas--The 34th Star

A Photographic Treasury of Kansas Issued in
Commemoration of the American Bicentennial

By Nyle H. Miller
and the staff of
The Kansas State Historical Society

Published
With the Support of
The Kansas State Legislature
and
The Kansas American Revolution Bicentennial Commission
by the
Kansas State Historical Society
Topeka, 1976

Copyright, 1976, by the
Kansas State Historical Society
Topeka

LC 76-4385
ISBN 0-87726-000-1

COVER PAINTING: Because of threats upon his life President-elect Abraham Lincoln traveled with a minimum of fanfare to his inaugural at Washington. He appeared briefly in Philadelphia on February 22, 1861, to raise for the first time at Independence Hall the flag of the United States bearing a 34th star, honoring Kansas the newest state. The historic scene was later depicted on canvas by J. L. G. Ferris under the title "Lincoln at Independence Hall."

END PAPERS: The Kansas region as depicted in the upper left of an Italian map of 1800 (back of front cover), and 61 years later the new state of Kansas as shown on a Mitchell "Map of Kansas, Nebraska, and Colorado . . ." (back of rear cover).

TABLE OF CONTENTS

Planet Earth . . ., Time, Land and Life	1
The First People—the Indians	2
The Spanish and French Interlude	4
Under the Stars and Stripes	8
Indian Reservations	9
Missions and Missionaries	10
Early Explorations	12
The Great Trails	14
Express and Stage Lines	18
The 1859 Gold Rush	20
United States Forts	22
The Indian Wars	23
The Struggle for Statehood	30
The Civil War	35
Settlement and Town Building	38
"Getting Around in Kansas"	54
The Arrival of the Iron Horse	60
Behold, the Gasoline Buggies	74
To the Skies	77
The Cowtown Frontier	80
Ranching and Agriculture	88
Kansas Mosaic	94
Doctor, Lawyer, Merchant	102
Culture on the Plains	112
They Made Their Marks	118
Happiness Is	126
Kansas Today	133
Picture Credits	147
Index	148

MAPS

The Kansas Region and the United States, 1800	back of front cover
Indian Locations	
Archeological Sites—Prehistoric	2
Nomadic and Village Tribes	6
Reservations	9
Louisiana Purchase	8
Routes of Early Explorers	12-13
Santa Fe and Oregon-California Trails	14-15
"Kansas Goldfields," Routes to, 1859	18-19
Pony Express, 1860-1861	19
Kansas Territory, 1854	30
State of Kansas, 1861	34
Chisholm and Other Cattle Trails From Texas	82-83
"Kansas, Nebraska and Colorado," 1861	back of rear cover

Planet Earth . . .

Which has been perpetually whirling in the Great Space orbit arranging its land and water masses into mountains, plains, valleys, rivers, seas, and oceans, for billions of years—give or take a few, as the carbon testers might say it.

Considering this vast expanse of Time it would seem that only this morning the first representatives of the Miracle of Humankind straggled in to the North American continent to commence their inhabiting of this portion of the Earth.

In the next few pages as we struggle to discover the first emerging of ourselves from the geological and vapor layers of the Earth it is humbling to realize that under many circumstances our identities are still obscured by the world's enveloping mists. For example an astronaut's picture (reproduced on this page) which arrived from the EROS Data Center of Sioux Falls, S. D., shows the United States and Kansas mostly under the clouds at the top right. Perhaps the U. S. location can be determined more easily through its Baja California handle in brown color, showing about one fourth of the way down from top center.

But we pass over this mention of the present, since the purpose of this book is to provide a brief report relating to life on Earth; namely that which our portions of Humankind discovered and experienced in the area now known as Kansas.

Time, Land and Life

History is never static, for seldom can its facts be determined and assembled to permit a final judgment. Much is yet to be discovered and understood before anything like a reasonably true accounting can be made of the story of this 200 x 400 mile section of planet Earth known as Kansas. Proof of a great part of this story must come from close studies of the earth itself, as layer upon layer is painstakingly scrutinized by geologists, paleontologists, and archeologists.

It has been estimated that the age of the earth is over four billion years. In that long, long period of time evidence indicates that this land of Kansas was inundated time and again by a variety of seas. The last of these is thought to have retreated some 60 million years ago. Many fossils, representative of those long-ago periods, have been recovered which provide a picture of prehistoric life which existed as the seas and land forms alternately asserted themselves. Remains of huge fish and aquatic dinosaurs have been found, as has evidence of five-toed horses, camels, rhino, saber-toothed tigers, and numerous other forms of life now long extinct.

Beginning some one and a half million years ago a series of glaciers moved down from the north, covering and scouring the land with mountains of ice. The largest of these glaciers entered what is now northeastern Kansas. During this Ice Age mammoths, mastodons, and early forms of bison, more commonly referred to as buffalo, roamed the countryside. Then as the ice receded there appeared on the continent new creatures—the first representatives of modern man.

An unusual erosion remnant in Gove county called "The Sphynx" (shown above) is part of the extensive Cretaceous deposits of western Kansas wherein can be found many remains of life forms which flourished during the misty eons of long, long ago.

For example, exhibited at the Sternberg Memorial Museum, Fort Hays Kansas State College, Hays, is a 14-foot Cretaceous fish *Xiphactinus molossus,* which shortly before its death had swallowed in one gulp a six-foot *Gillicus arcuatus*! The pair as shown was collected in 1952 in Gove county.

And this 10-foot short-necked plesiosaur skeleton, said to be the most nearly complete of its kind yet found, is also from the chalk beds of western Kansas.

The evolving buffalo was by far the most important of these living creatures to make the transition from that distant age, drifting stolidly into the modern era.

The First People

Paleo-Indian dart points, collected from the Kansas river valley.

The Hunters

Migrating from Asia thousands of years ago, the first people to arrive on the North American continent were the hunters. Probably they crossed where the Bering Sea now is, as did many of the animals they pursued, on a wide land bridge then linking the two continents. Chipped stone dart points found with the bones of now extinct animals prove their early presence. Archeologists term these first people the Paleo-Indians.

Changes in climate through later thousands of years altered the varieties of animals and plants as well as human technology. By approximately 5,000 B.C. what is known as the Archaic period had begun. The peoples of that time existed not only by hunting animals but also by making use of edible plants, roots, and seeds. In small populations, probably representing extended families, they moved frequently in search of food.

An Archaic fired clay effigy head found near Council Grove.

Burned stones in an Archaic campfire some 5,000 years old. This hearth was found deeply buried in the Neosho river valley near Council Grove.

SOME PREHISTORIC ARCHEOLOGICAL SITES OF KANSAS

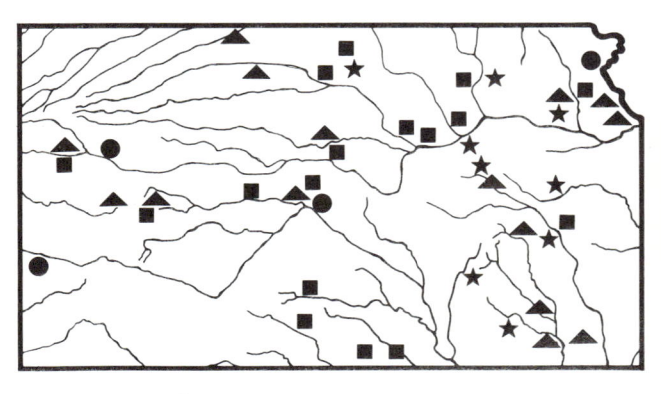

● Paleo-Indian, 10,000-5,000 B. C.
★ Archaic, 5,000 B. C.-1 A. D.
▲ Plains Woodland, 1-950 A. D.
■ Plains Farmer, 950-1500 A. D.

The Farmers

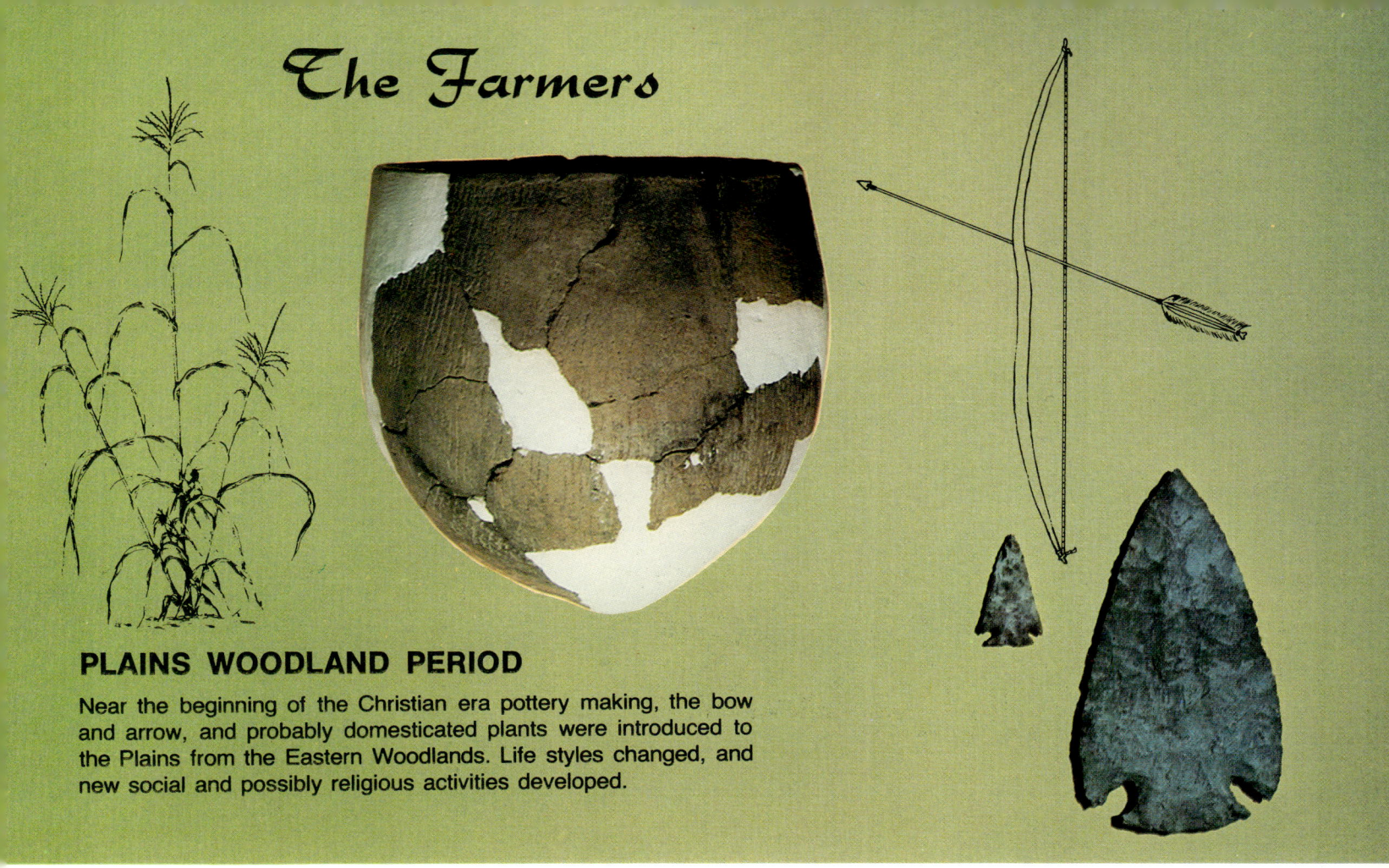

PLAINS WOODLAND PERIOD

Near the beginning of the Christian era pottery making, the bow and arrow, and probably domesticated plants were introduced to the Plains from the Eastern Woodlands. Life styles changed, and new social and possibly religious activities developed.

Earthlodge.

PLAINS FARMERS

By 1000 A.D. the Plains Farmer era began. Gardening supplemented hunting and gathering. More permanent dwellings such as the earthlodge were used, and in time villages appeared along terrace tops adjacent to streams.

Prehistoric earthlodge floor excavated near Minneapolis.

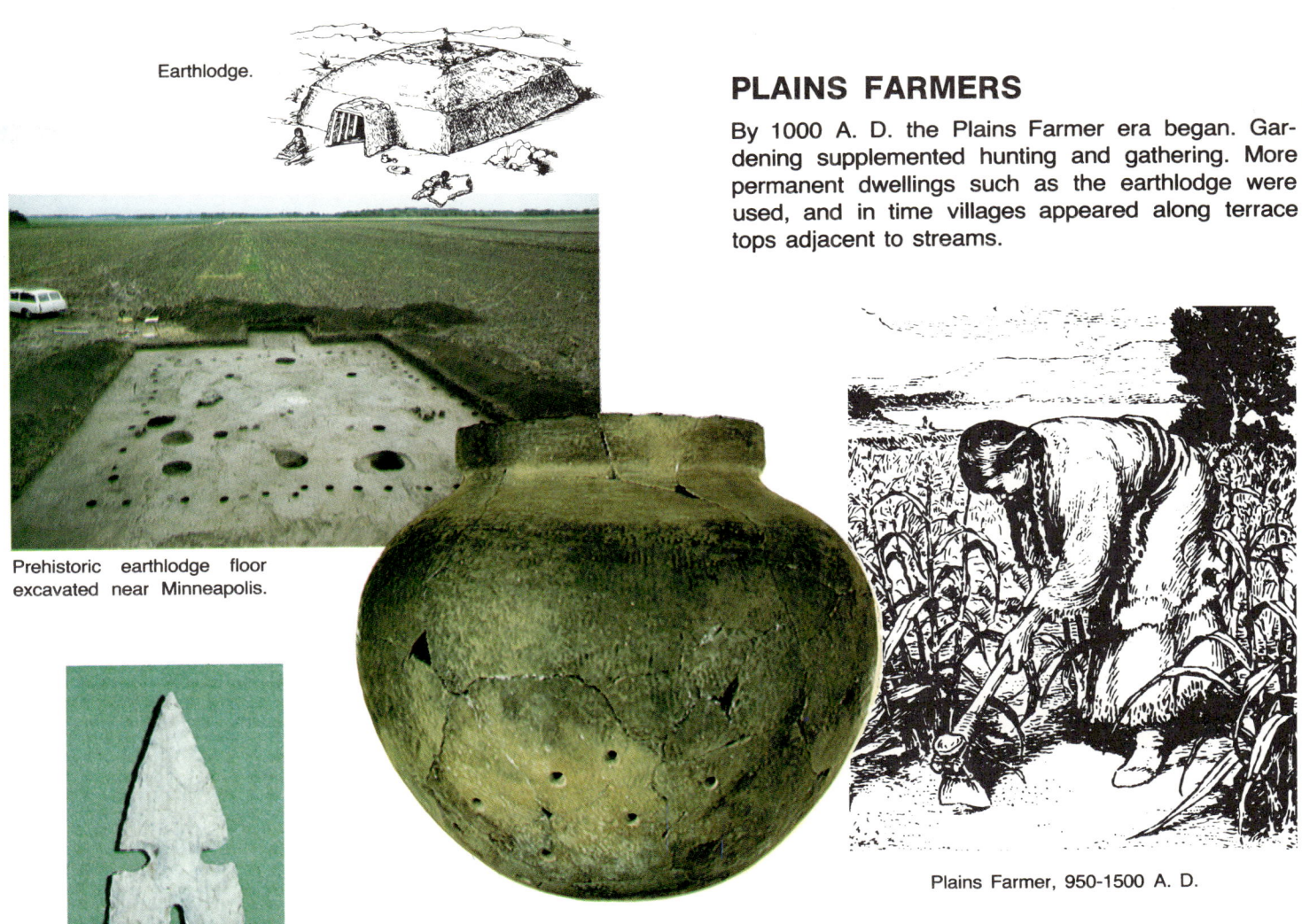

Plains Farmer, 950-1500 A.D.

The Spanish and French Interlude
(1541-1803)

The first Europeans to reach present Kansas were the Spanish. In 1541 an expedition of some 40 men led by Francisco Vasquez de Coronado came from the Southwest in search of the fabled land of Quivira. Though they traveled as far as central Kansas and visited extensive villages of bands later known as the Wichita Indians, they found no gold or other wealth. Within the next 250 years other Spanish expeditions followed, including those of Leyva y Bonilla and Humaña, Oñate, Archuleta, Ulibarri, and Villasur.

Later French traders moved in from the East to barter with the Indians for furs to please the fashion centers of Europe. Among them were Du Tisné, Bourgmont, and the Mallet brothers. As the Europeans met various Plains Indians they gave names to the tribes and began to document their land and way of life, thus providing the first written records about the peoples of the area that became Kansas.

A sword blade believed to have belonged to one of Coronado's officers was found in 1886 in present Greeley county. Because of the several Spanish expeditions into present western Kansas it is not surprising that other blades have been uncovered in recent years.

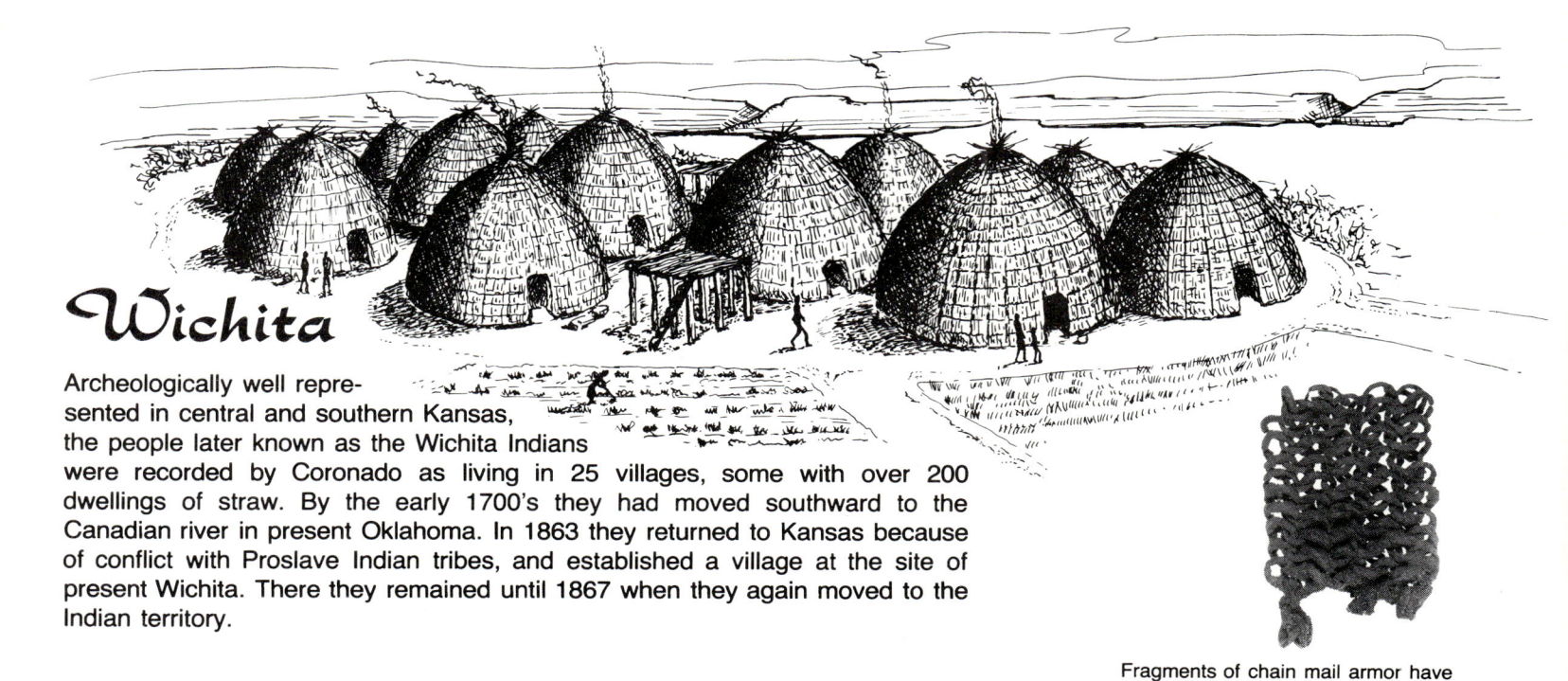

Wichita

Archeologically well represented in central and southern Kansas, the people later known as the Wichita Indians were recorded by Coronado as living in 25 villages, some with over 200 dwellings of straw. By the early 1700's they had moved southward to the Canadian river in present Oklahoma. In 1863 they returned to Kansas because of conflict with Proslave Indian tribes, and established a village at the site of present Wichita. There they remained until 1867 when they again moved to the Indian territory.

Fragments of chain mail armor have been found in Wichita village sites in Rice and McPherson counties.

Cuartelejo Apache

Early Spanish expeditions met Plains Apache groups which they described as existing like the Arabs, using dogs to transport their belongings, and living off the meat of the buffalo. Twice in the middle and late 1600's pueblo Indians, fleeing from the Spanish, took refuge at an Apache rancheria believed to have been in the present Scott county area. That place became known as El Cuartelejo and the Apache there as the Cuartelejo band. The Apache were driven from the High Plains by Comanche marauders a short time later. An artist's sketch of El Cuartelejo pueblo appears at the right.

Restored ruins of El Cuartelejo pueblo in Lake Scott State Park near Scott City.

The Pawnee Indian Village Museum near Republic.

Pawnee

Though they lived much as the prehistoric earthlodge peoples of central Kansas, the Pawnee are linguistically related to the Wichita. North-central and western Kansas was the area of seasonal tribal buffalo hunts, and French traders came among the Pawnee in the early 1700's. While their large semipermanent villages are usually found in the Nebraska area, the site of a Republican band village also exists in northwest Republic county, Kansas. There a modern museum illustrates the Pawnee way of life through displays like the diorama pictured at the left.

Kansa

The Kansa Indians, for whom the state was named, and the Osage were Siouan speaking tribes believed to have moved in from the east around the middle of the 17th century. Bourgmont visited the Kansa in 1724 at their village located where Doniphan now stands. Later they moved south and west to various village sites along the Kansas river. Though a small tribe they warred with the village and nomadic tribes to the north and west.

A Kansa dog dance was sketched in a lodge just east of present Manhattan on August 24, 1819, by Samuel Seymour of the Maj. S. H. Long expedition. It was published in 1822, the first drawing, as far as is known, ever printed relating to what is now Kansas.

White Plume, a Kansa chief, about 1821.

Osage

An Osage warrior whose tribe was first recorded on the Osage river in present Missouri. By 1820 the Osage began to move west and south and in 1825 were ceded reservation lands in present southeast Kansas. Their seasonal buffalo hunts later extended into central Kansas.

Some of the early tribes of Kansas

- PAWNEE 1500's-1800's
- CHEYENNE & ARAPAHOE 1800's
- KANSA 1600's-1800's
- CUARTELEJO APACHE 1600's-1700's
- WICHITA (QUIVIRA) 1500's-1700's
- OSAGE 1600's-1800's
- COMANCHE KIOWA, KIOWA APACHE 1700's-1800's

A Time of Change

Although the evolution of the horse in this land some millions of years ago has been established, the animal had become extinct here by 6,000 B. C. In the 1500's the horse was reintroduced to the continent by the Spanish, and eventually reached the Plains Indians in such numbers as to completely change their way of living. Previously, hunting on foot had limited the Indians to stalking or entrapment, but with the horse came the chase and greater mobility among the now teeming herds of buffalo. The horse truly opened an exciting chapter in the history of the early American West.

The Horse Nomads

As the tribes became more mobile they sometimes abandoned their old ways and moved or extended their territories into the High Plains. Maps and notebooks of the explorers now begin to include such names as Comanche, Kiowa, Kiowa Apache, Cheyenne, and Arapaho. Utilizing the tipi as portable homes the Indians could range over thousands of square miles in their hunts.

To the Indian the horse was not only wealth but the means of wealth. Raids upon other tribes for horses were common. Feats of mounted daring brought great status to individual warriors, especially when they associated into bands like the celebrated Dog Soldiers who were described by Henry Stanley in 1867 as "the elite of the Cheyenne nation, who look with scorn and contempt upon all other bands." The hide painting to the left depicts a raid by Kansa Indians upon a Pawnee village to secure horses. Intending to ride home with their prizes, the Kansa were killed by mounted Pawnee defenders.

Under the Stars and Stripes

After some 250 years of being trampled on by the Spanish and French, who couldn't fully make up their minds as to her virtues, "Kansas" suddenly, in 1803, became the property of that new nation being formed to the east, the United States of America. For approximately $15 million President Thomas Jefferson purchased all of the French interest in Lousiana territory, which stretched from New Orleans to the present Canadian border and contained much of what later became 13 American states. Included was present Kansas except its southwest corner, and title to that portion was finally acquired in 1850.

The first American exploration of the new purchase was led by Meriwether Lewis and William Clark with a party consisting of some 45 men in a 55-foot keelboat and two pirogues. They set foot in present Kansas at the mouth of the Kaw river on June 26, 1804, on their way up the Missouri. On July 4, in the vicinity of present Atchison, they celebrated Independence day, the first such observance in Kansas. More permanently they called a nearby stream Independence creek, which name it bears today. After pushing across to the Pacific ocean the expedition again touched Kansas as it returned down the river in 1806.

The wide Missouri river (here pictured bordering Doniphan county) was the Way West for many early explorers and trappers, including the first Americans, Lewis and Clark, who traveled this route in 1804.

Meriwether Lewis

William Clark

> **LOUISIANA** BOUGHT BUT NOT YET PAID FOR. WHO PAYS FOR IT?
>
> At length we hear *Louisiana* is bought. For what? To secure the right of deposit. Better affert our old Treaty right as derived from *Spain*, than buy new rights:—Especially to buy them with the millions that are wanted to provide ships and troops to secure them—especially too, let it be added, by giving thofe millions to the only government that has rendered or that will make that right and all our rights unfafe.
>
> We are to give money of which we have too little for land of which we already have too much—We expofe our want of fpirit, and aggravate our want of ftrength.
>
> There ought to be fome balance in the Union; as before hinted, this unexplored empire, of the fize of four or five European kingdoms will deftroy that—will drain our people away from the purfuit of a better hufbandry, and from manufactures and commerce.
>
> Can an Empire fo unwieldly, fo nearly uncivilized, that will for a century or two require fuch heavy charge and contribute fo little towards defraying any part of it, will it be, can it be fubject to *one* Government?—And if it fhould, will that Government be republican? Does it not threaten to fever, and if not to fever to fubjugate the Union? Will not thefe new mountaineer ftates claim power and refift taxes? Give us Reprefentatives in Congrefs who will have power over the men of the eaft; flaves over free whites, but do not lay direct taxes in the fame proportion. Will not this be their language, as it ever has been that of *Virginia*?
>
> A momentous crifis is at hand. Ever fince 1789, the confumers who pay moft are from *Pennfylvania*, eaftward. The inhabitants who have coft moft to the United States Treafury, are thofe who live Weft from *Pennfylvania*. Ours are the burdens, theirs the benefits.
>
> JULY 12.   FABRICIUS.

Excerpted from column one, page two, of the *Columbian Centinel & Massachusetts Federalist*, Boston, Mass., July 13, 1803.

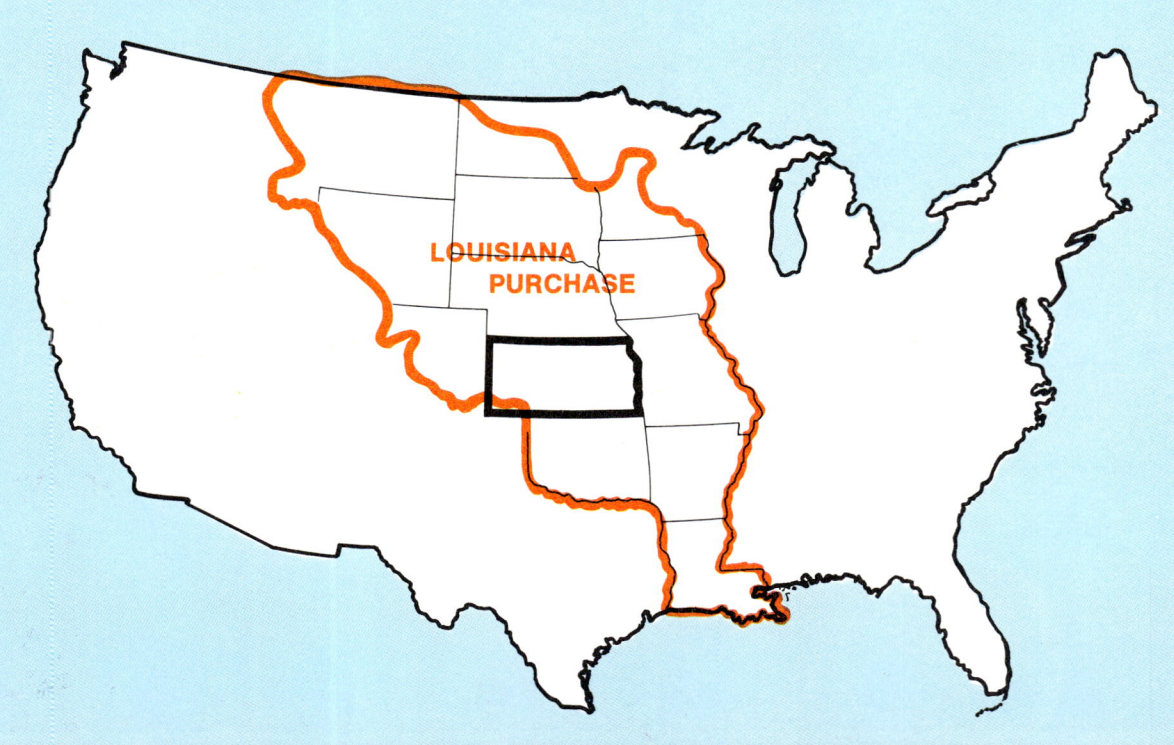

Clay figurine, steel arrowhead and brass bell recovered by archeologists from a mid-19th century Pottawatomie site near Topeka.

The Reservations

The United States developed in the early decades of the 1800's a plan to remove Indian tribes then living in the Eastern portion of the country to selected reservations west of the Mississippi river. The presence of the Indians in the East was becoming a barrier to the expansion of the new nation, as well as a source of continual trouble. But the professed reasons for removal were the growing scarcity of game upon which the tribes depended and the association of the Indians with immoral whites which might ultimately lead to their destruction.

In the region that became eastern Kansas, reservations for a score of these Emigrant tribes were laid out (see map below). Since the Kansa and Osage already had been more or less in possession of that land, treaties were made in 1825 to diminish their holdings to make room for the Emigrant tribes. Some of these tribes made their government-enforced removals with relative success while others endured much suffering with considerable loss of life and property. A few tribes were fortunate in being better led by concerned and efficient whites, but for many their relocation brought tragic consequences, partly due to the differences in environment and resulting problems of mental and physical adaptation. By 1840 some 100,000 Eastern Indians had been removed to what is now the eastern portion of the Nebraska-Kansas-Oklahoma area.

By 1850 Indian tribes in "Kansas," including the new arrivals, numbered 27. But in "Kansas" they still were a barrier to westward expansion. Hardly had the tribes been resettled before plans were started to relocate as many as possible in the area south of Kansas then known as Indian territory. These moves took place in the 1850's to the 1870's and today only remnants of the Pottawatomie, Iowa, Sac and Fox, and Kickapoo Indian nations remain.

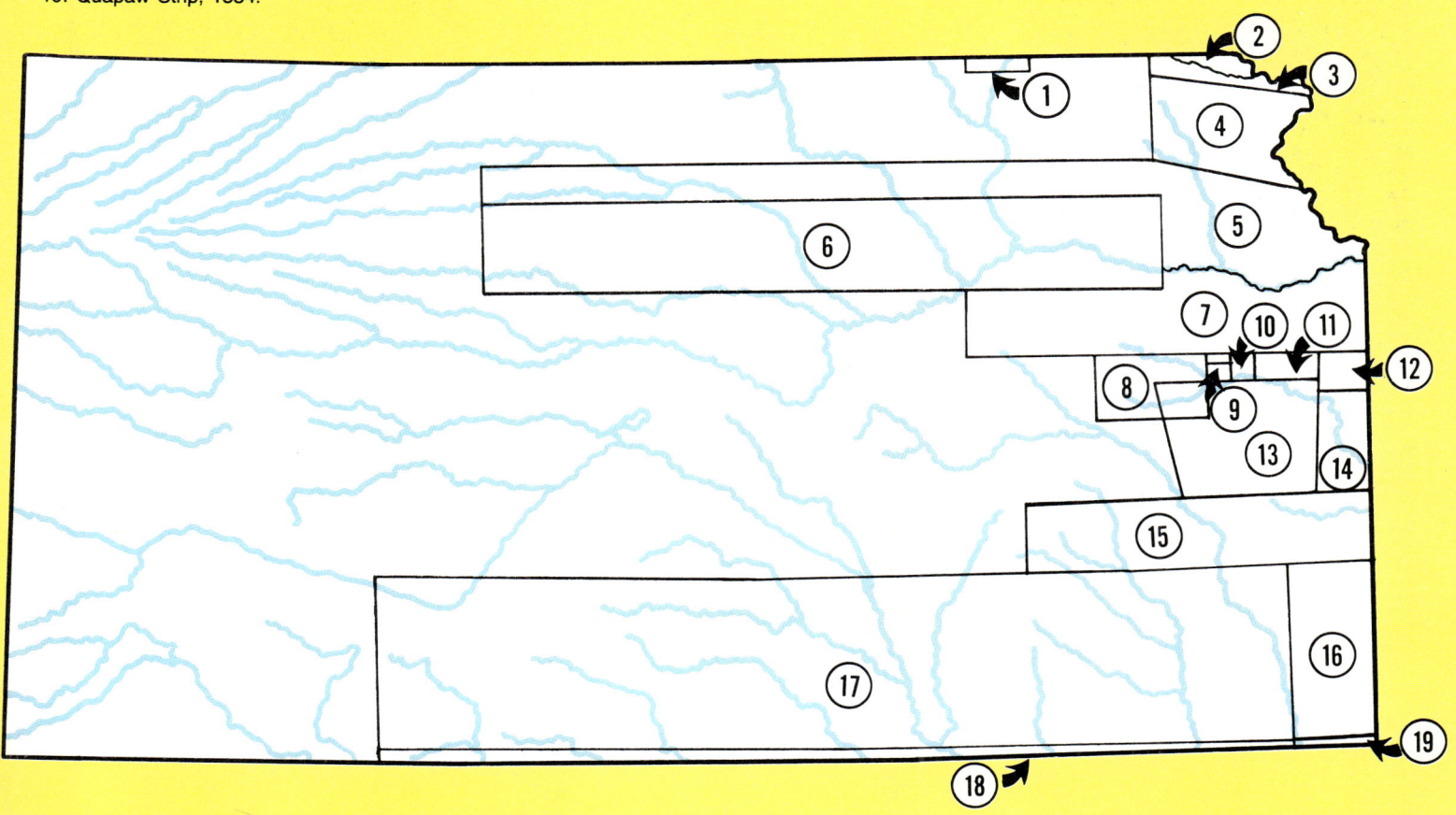

INDIAN RESERVATIONS—
In territory included in Kansas, 1846.
1. Oto and Missouri. 2. Iowa, 1837. 3. Sac and Fox of Missouri, 1837. 4. Kickapoo Reserve, established under treaty of 1833. 5. Delaware Reserve and Outlet, established under treaty of 1831. 6. Kansa Reserve, established under treaty of 1825. 7. Shawnee Reserve, established by treaty of 1825. 8. Sac and Fox of Mississippi, 1843. 9. Chippewa Reserve, 1830. 10. Ottawa Reserve, 1832. 11. Peoria and Kaskaskia, 1833. 12. Wea and Piankeshaw, 1833. 13. Pottawatomie Reserve, established under treaty of 1837. 14. Miami Reserve, 1839 and 1841. 15. New York Indian Lands, conveyed under treaty of 1838. 16. Cherokee Neutral Lands, conveyed under treaty of 1835. 17. Osage Reserve, established by treaty of 1825. (The western boundary, originally the dotted line, was arbitrarily extended by the surveyors to the old Mexican line.) 18. Cherokee Strip, conveyed under treaty of 1835. 19. Quapaw Strip, 1834.

Missions and Missionaries

As the removal of Eastern Indians to new reservations in the West began in 1830 the tribes were accompanied or quickly followed by missionaries of several churches who hoped to provide religious and educational services. Even earlier, in 1824, the first Indian mission in what is now Kansas had been established among the Osage in present Neosho county by Presbyterian and associated denominations, but it was discontinued in 1829. Perhaps the most successful, in numbers of Indians enrolled and buildings erected, was Thomas Johnson's Shawnee Methodist Mission and Manual Labor School. Its three remaining buildings are today one of Kansas' most interesting and attractive historic sites. Nearby was another mission-school to the Shawnee, operated by Baptists, where in 1834 Jotham Meeker, the first printer in Kansas, began publishing and distributing books and religious tracts in Indian languages. Among other denominations operating schools and missions for various tribes were the Friends, Catholics and Moravians.

Isaac McCoy, a Baptist missionary who worked with several Eastern Indian tribes, accompanied their representatives in the late 1820's to select lands in Kansas. He and his son, John, surveyed many of the new reservations.

The Rev. Thomas Johnson, long-time superintendent of the Shawnee Methodist Mission and Manual Labor School.

Shawnee Methodist Mission, originally located in 1830 in present Wyandotte county, was moved to Johnson county in 1839. The East building, the second of the permanent buildings, was constructed in 1841 and contained a chapel and school and lodging rooms for teachers and children, both white and Indian. The present-day location of this state-owned historic site, a National Historic Landmark, is 3403 W. 53rd Street, Fairway, Kan.

An artist's rendition of the Baptist mission to the Pottawatomie at the west edge of present Topeka near I-70. The building, dating from 1849, was later converted to use as a barn and stables. It is now owned by the state of Kansas.

Samuel Irvin and his wife Eliza established a Presbyterian mission to the Iowa, Sac and Fox Indians in present Doniphan county in 1837. A portion of the main building, erected in 1846 and located on K-136, just off US-36 east of Highland, is now a state-owned museum administered by the Kansas State Historical Society.

The Catholic mission to the Pottawatomie was established at present St. Marys in 1848.

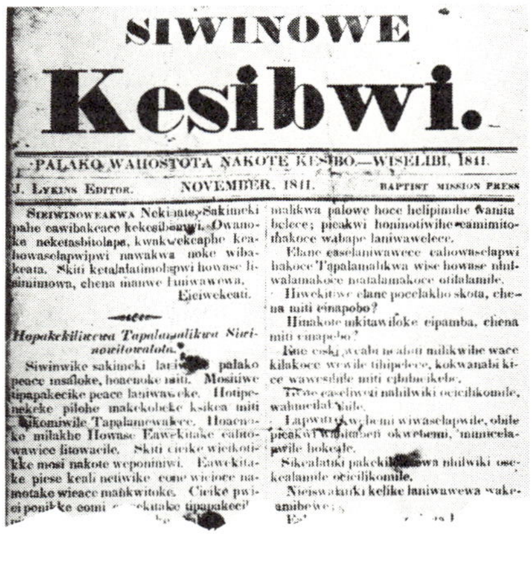

Siwinowe Kesibwi, which in English means *Shawnee Sun*, was established by Jotham Meeker at the Shawnee Baptist mission in 1835, the first newspaper published in "Kansas" and the "first Indian language periodical published in the United States." The little paper was issued at intervals under the editorship of Johnston Lykins, another Baptist missionary. Its circulation never exceeded 150 copies or so, and it ceased publication in 1844. Only one copy of this pioneer newspaper is known to exist.

Jotham Meeker, in addition to being the first printer in Kansas, developed an English orthography so that Indian languages could be printed with standard type.

11

Early Explorations

Zebulon M. Pike

Stephen H. Long

John C. Fremont

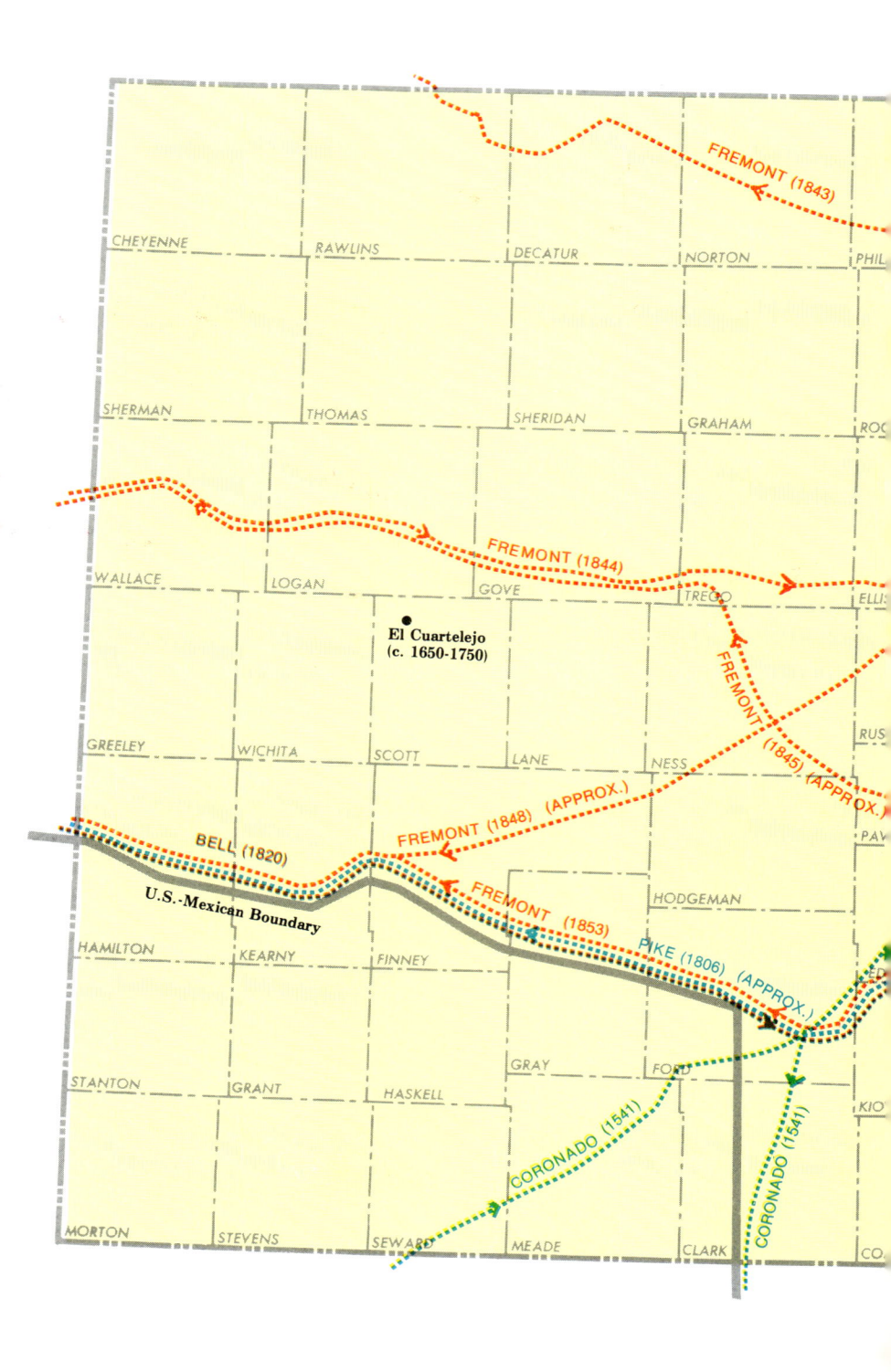

Shown on this map are the routes of several noted explorers and travelers who crossed the "Kansas" area. The march of Coronado, first white man known to have entered the region, is approximate, for evidence is too meager to pinpoint his precise course. He is believed to have entered "Kansas" near present Liberal, then traveled northeast to, and along, the Arkansas river to the Great Bend from where he swung east into present McPherson and southern Saline counties. His vain search for the fabulous gold of Quivira is known to every school child, but he was successful in gaining information about the country and in establishing Spanish claim to it. Other Spanish expeditions, and several French, are not shown for lack of specific data, including visits of soldiers from both nations to El Cuartelejo, the 17th century Indian pueblo whose ruins may still be seen in Scott county, and the travels of Bourgmont who in 1724 moved as far west as present Saline or Ellsworth counties. The exact location of Fort Cavagnial, a French fur-trading outpost in present Leavenworth county, also remains unknown.

American exploration began with Lewis and Clark, who touched the northeastern corner of "Kansas" as they traveled up the Missouri in 1804 and down in 1806. At sunrise, near present Atchison, they observed the 4th of July, 1804, by firing a swivel gun—a small cannon—from their keelboat. Later they named Independence creek and closed the day with another cannon blast.

Next came Cpt. Zebulon Pike, the first American directed to examine the southern portion of the Louisiana Purchase, who headed west across the Kansas prairies in 1806. He detoured into southern Nebraska, then turned south again to the Great Bend of the Arkansas. From that point Lt. James B. Wilkinson was sent southeast with a small party to inspect the valley of the Arkansas. Pike himself continued westward to discover the Rocky mountain peak that bears his name, and to the headwaters of the Rio Grande. There he was captured by the Spanish, who thought, probably with some justification, that he was a spy, and held prisoner in Mexico for six months. His scientific notes were confiscated but some data secreted in the barrels of his men's rifles escaped detection and survived to insure the historical success of the expedition.

The major portion of Stephen H. Long's expedition of 1819 got no farther into "Kansas" than the

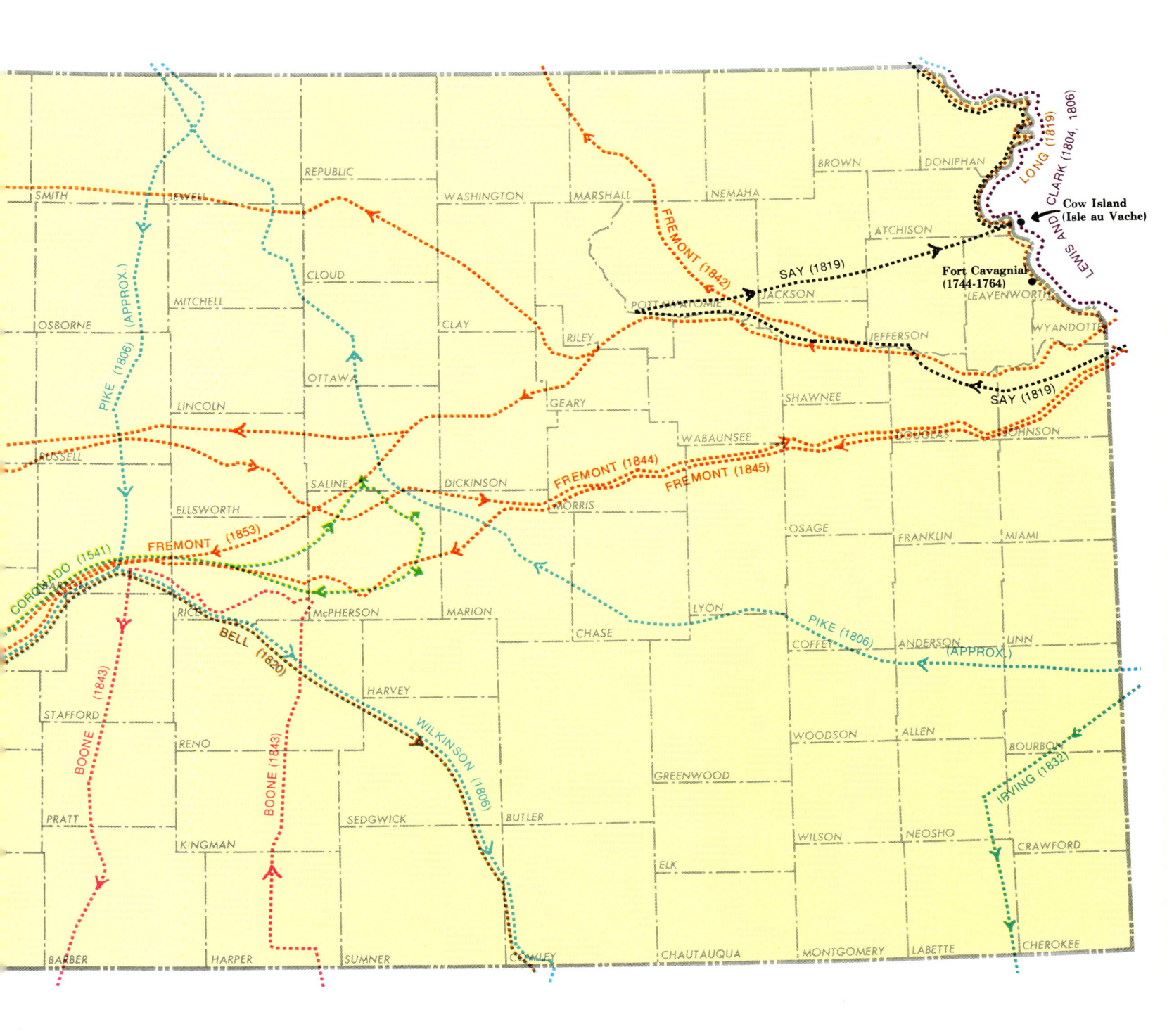

Missouri river, but two of its detachments did accomplish substantial reconnoitering of the interior. Thomas Say, the expedition's zoologist, led a party up the Kansas river as far as the Blue, where hostile Pawnee stole their supplies and scattered their pack horses. Say then gave up his projected journey north to the Platte and rejoined the main expedition on the Missouri near present Atchison. In the summer of 1820, when the expedition was in present Colorado, Cpt. John Bell (accompanied by Say and others) was sent east along the Arkansas river, which formed part of the northern boundary of Mexico. While rounding the Great Bend of the Arkansas on a hot August 9, Say reported: "The soil of the afternoon journey was a deep fine white sand, which rendered the traveling very laborious . . . and affected the sight, by the great glare of light which it so freely reflected. The chief produce of these tracts of unmixed sand is the sunflower, often the dense and almost exclusive occupant." (Say's account, printed in 1823, was the first published reference to the sunflower which became the official "state flower" of Kansas 80 years later.) Although Say and the other Long scientists gathered considerable information their unfamiliarity with the Plains led them to conclude that the region was "almost wholly unfit for cultivation, and of course uninhabitable. . . ." Major Long's map subsequently labeled the area the "Great American Desert."

Between 1842 and 1853 John C. Fremont, peripatetic soldier and politician, traveled thousands of miles between the Missouri river and the Pacific coast. He crossed Kansas several times, collecting data on flora, fauna and topography, and his published maps and reports gave the American public a deeper understanding of the Plains and mountains of the West. Fremont was a better judge of the prairie potential than either Pike or Long, believing that the "Kansas" area had great agricultural possibilities.

Among others who had opportunity to look at the country were writer Washington Irving who crossed the southeastern corner of "Kansas" in 1832 and later briefly described the journey in his *A Tour on the Prairies,* and Cpt. Nathan Boone, son of Daniel, who circled through south-central Kansas in 1843.

The Great Trails

Two of the most important trails in the nation's history were the roads which led to Santa Fe and to California and Oregon. They became the ties that firmly cemented the American East with the developing West, and the traffic pulsing through these arteries year-by-year provided a never-failing indicator of the strength of the great Westward movement.

The Santa Fe Trail

Nearly two-thirds of the Santa Fe trail's 780-mile route lay through Kansas. It stretched from Missouri river towns opposite northeast Kansas, southwest across the entire state and on to the trade marts of Santa Fe. William Becknell, using pack animals, is credited with opening the route in 1821. The next year he traveled with wagons, and thereafter, for half a century, countless wagon trains passed over the trail engaged in commerce with the Spanish Southwest. Along the trail also passed the troops and supplies for forts, for pacifying and providing goods to the Indian tribes, and for the Mexican war, and finally the emigrants to the new American territory in the Southwest.

Many roads joined the main Santa Fe trail in eastern "Kansas." Wet and dry routes converged near Dodge City, while to the west other branches dropped off to the Cimarron river, a hazardous short-cut to Santa Fe. Roads to Santa

Christopher "Kit" Carson

Bennet Riley

Francis X. Aubry

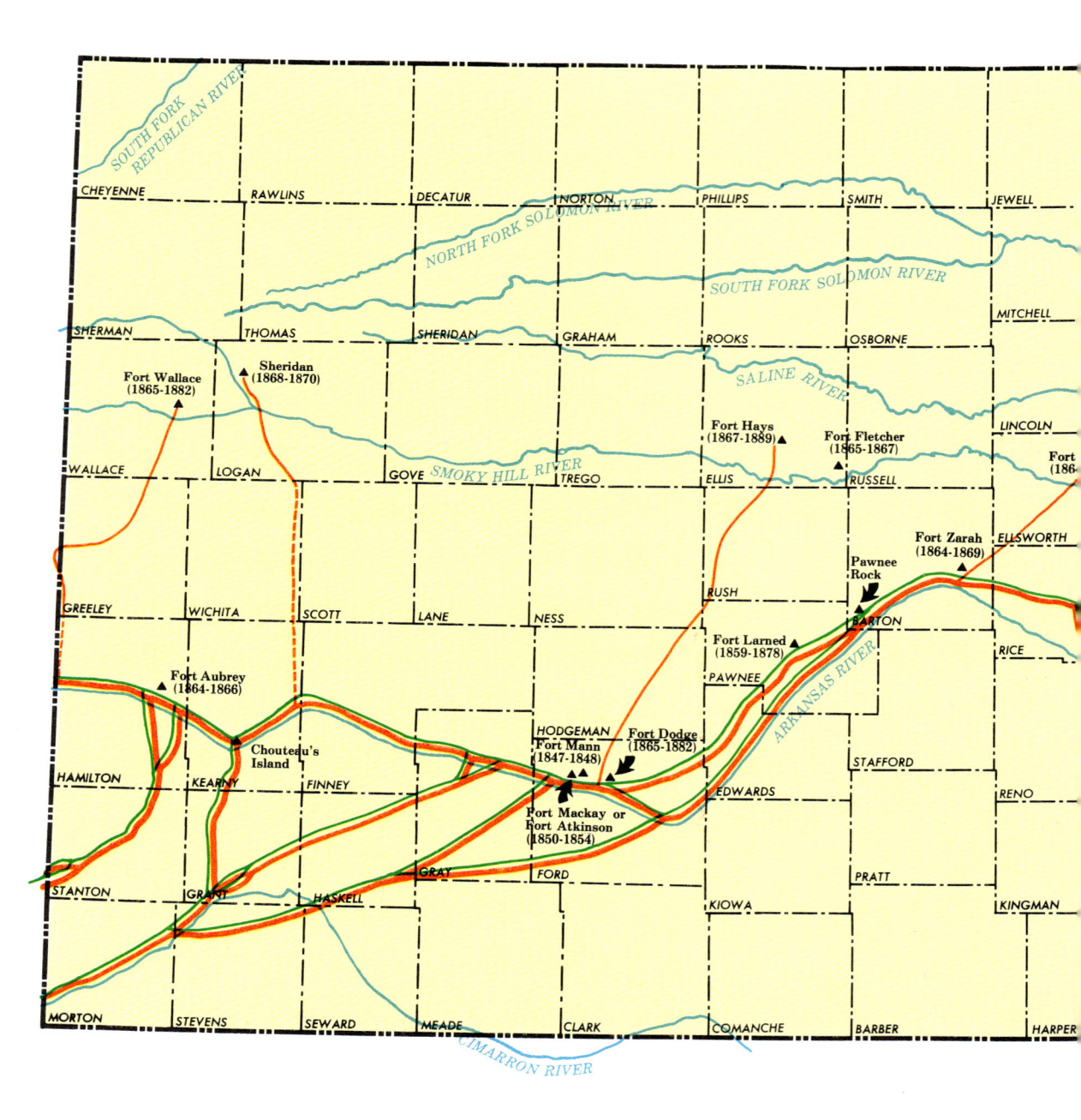

Fe (shown on this map in red with the main routes in heavier lines) suggest that almost anyone who wanted to go there had only to face that way and start. Red lines dropping down from forts and towns in west central Kansas also show some of the feeder roads which developed when these places, in the latter 1860's, were end-of-track towns for the west-building Union Pacific railroad, Eastern Division (called the Kansas Pacific after March 3, 1869).

Well-known Americans who earned their spurs in the early development of the trail included Christopher "Kit" Carson, who made his first trip to Santa Fe in 1826 as a runaway boy of 17. Bvt. Maj. Bennet Riley, for whom Fort Riley was later named, with 200 of the Sixth U. S. infantry, escorted westbound traders in the early summer of 1829 to a crossing on the Arkansas river near Chouteau's Island in present Kearny county (on the then Mexican boundary). There he and his soldiers tarried for several weeks awaiting the return of the caravan from Santa Fe. On October 12, 1829, the eastbound traders under protection of Mexican Col. Jose Antonio Viscarra, met the Americans at the crossing. A great feast was prepared and enjoyed by over 500 persons, while oxen and more than "2,000 horses, mules, [and] jacks, which kept up an incessant braying," grazed nearby.

One of the most interesting figures in the history of the trail was the "Skimmer of the Plains," Santa Fe trader Francis X. Aubry, who must have worn out the fastest horses in the West as he continually set new trail-riding records. On May 28, 1848, he rode into Independence, Mo., after having traveled "the 780-mile length of Santa Fe trail in 'the incredible short space of **eight days and ten hours!!!!'**," yet he topped it the following September 17 when he arrived at Independence **"five days and 16 hours"** out of Santa Fe.

The Oregon-California Trail

Emigrant traffic over the developing 2,000-mile route to Oregon and California began in 1841. Many of these thousands of travelers, like those headed for Santa Fe, also funneled through Missouri river towns opposite Kansas. However, the departure season for those enroute to the Far West was shorter since they needed to follow the greening grass if forage were to be had for their livestock, and to cross the Sierras before the frosts changed to snow.

Two of the great Oregon-California routes through Kansas started from Independence and St. Joseph, Mo. Other varying routes joined with one or the other of these main trails. At a point west of the Marshall-Washington county line these main roads from Independence and St. Joe met and continued as one, crossing the Kansas-Nebraska border not far from the present state-owned Pony Express station near Hanover. Roads through Kansas to Oregon-California, delineated on the map in green, are mostly centered in northeastern Kansas although, as shown, some travelers chose the Santa Fe trail route before heading north along the eastern slope of the Rocky mountains.

Many persons find maps deeply fascinating. But how much more interesting they become when reasons for the development of the routes and what possessed the travelers who made them are known. For example, the junction of the Independence and St. Joe routes of the Oregon-California trail about ten miles west of Marysville seems of no great consequence on the map. Yet if one could have stood there with emigrant W. G. Johnston on May 10, 1849, the year of the Great Gold Rush to California, this is what he would have seen, as described by Johnston: "From an elevation at the point of intersection we had an extensive view, and in looking behind over the road just traveled [from Independence], or back over the St. Joseph road, or forward over that to be taken; for an indefinite number of miles, there seemed to be an unending stream of emigrant trains, whilst in the still farther distance along these lines could be seen great clouds of dust, indicating that yet others of these immense caravans were on the move. It was a sight which once seen can never be forgotten; it seemed as if the whole family of man had set its face westward."

It was journey's end for this '49er—S. M. Marshall—on the Oregon-California trail near present Westmoreland.

15

Traveling the Trails

Only a small fraction of the newsworthy items reaching the public from travelers following the Santa Fe and the Oregon-California trails through Kansas was concerned with so-called Indian depredations, or attacks by either side. They did occur, of course. Though the Indian was not always unfriendly when encountered by whites, it was wise for each never to let his guard down. Examples of other types of newsbits include these:

The Santa Fe Trail

1843, June 30.—In a boundary dispute between the Republic of Texas and the United States Cpt. Philip St. George Cooke, with 190 dragoons and two howitzers, while following the Santa Fe trail about 10 miles east of present Dodge City, saw some 100 Texans under Col. Jacob Snively camped across the river claiming they were in Texas. Cooke thought not, so captured and partly disarmed them to prevent their preying further on the Santa Fe trade. [p. 487.]

1847, June 22, 23.—Camped on the Pawnee Fork near present Larned were several wagon trains waiting for floodwaters to recede. Around one wagon were any quantity of gaping men, and "a **whitewoman**—a real whitewoman!" [p. 693.]

1848, May 12.—"The road from [Council Grove east to Independence, Mo.] . . . is almost one continued encampment of Santa Fe and Chihuahua traders." [p. 750.]

1850, August 3.—Army recruits destined for Santa Fe duty brought the cholera with them as they debarked at Fort Leavenworth. While set off in a camp near the fort one of them wrote: "Cholera raging to an awful extent among us. Men at active pursuits one day . . .; the next day they are a loathsome mass, thrown coffinless into the yawning pit. We wrap 4 to 5 daily in their blankets, and throw their remains in the ground with a blessing or a prayer. No stone marks their last resting place . . . desertions continued in gangs from 3 to 8." [p. 955.]

1852, August 8.—Ox team freighting was described by a traveler: "The average travel per day with six yoke is from eighteen to twenty miles. They return empty with five yoke in each and make twenty to twenty-five miles in a day." [p. 1115.]

1852, September 7.—Four Sisters of Loretto accompanied the Rt. Rev. John B. Lamy to New Mexico in the summer of 1852 to found a boarding school mission. While encamped near Fort Atkinson, west of present Dodge City, about 400 Indians, non-hostile, surrounded the wagons, which was a terrifying experience for the Sisters. [p. 1116.]

1852, September 8.—A Chihuahua-bound traveler between present Larned and Kinsley reported that "the buffalo herds formed a close line at least eight miles long upon the northern heights. Doubtless this herd, which surrounded us for a week whilst traveling, consisted of millions of animals, and formed one body, journeying along in company. I must, with my own eyes, have seen hundreds of thousands." [p. 1102.]

A vast sky and the seemingly endless Kansas prairie merge in the distance in this depiction of the Santa Fe trail by Henry Worrall, a 19th century Topeka painter and illustrator.

Council Grove, once the westernmost outfitting point on the trail, for years enjoyed a thriving trade with passing caravans. The two street scenes (above, in the 1860's; below, some years later) show it as a typical Kansas frontier town.

"Crossing the Kansas," by Western artist Alfred Jacob Miller, shows an American Fur Company caravan fording the river above present Lawrence in 1837 on its way to the Rockies.

The Oregon-California Trail

1849, May.—[Leaving Fort Leavenworth and after crossing Wolf creek in present Doniphan county on May 22 we on May 23] "came into a road as large as any public highway in the United States, leading from St. Joseph and Weston.... Large trains were coming in from all points on the Missouri river on trails intersecting this great highway.... All these trails followed ridges, which placed the wagons frequently in such position that they seemed to be crossing the prairies in every direction . . . they looked at a distance not unlike vessels on the wide ocean steering for different parts of the globe." [p. 865.]

1850, May 6.—Just across the Missouri river from St. Joseph in the midst of the "Kansas" wilderness "there is the hum and bustle of a great city. Not less than 10,000 emigrants are encamped in the woods on the opposite bank. The poor Kickapoos . . . gaze upon the crowd and their doings with wonderment." [p. 920.]

1850, May 12.—Blue river crossing at present Marysville: "Here we found a large city of tents, and preaching. There were probably 2000 men camped within two miles of the crossing; and here we found wagons broken down last year, with irons of those burnt. . . . we found some last year's graves, besides the usual amount of dead horses. . . ." [p. 924.]

1852, April 26.—Jotham Meeker, at his Ottawa Baptist mission east of present Ottawa, wrote: "7 or 800 Cattle & perhaps 50 wagons pass for California—for 5 or 6 days past great numbers have passed us. Am compelled to watch my Cattle to prevent their being driven off." [p. 1078.]

1852, Spring.—"When we reached the prairie [wrote emigrant Theodore E. Potter in present eastern Doniphan county] we found that all the emigrants who had crossed the [Missouri] river during the five previous days had gone into camp waiting for the rain to cease. . . . It was a grand sight to look over the prairie as far as the eye could discern and see the new white-covered wagons and tents clustered here and there and the great number of horses and cattle, scattered in every direction, trying to get a bite of the short spring grass that had just started to grow. It was estimated at the time that at least 10,000 emigrants were camped within a distance of ten miles of this point. . . . The morning of the eighth of May brought us good weather and the entire body of people and animals formed a great procession and started on the way. Previous to this time there had been but one trail over which the wagons could pass. But 10,000 people starting from the same locality on the same day made it necessary for more trails, which were very easily made on the open prairie, excepting when we came to a stream that had to be bridged. During the first day's march there were at least 12 roads for 12 teams abreast." [pp. 1088, 1089.]

1852, June.—The Oregon-California trail, between Fort Kearny and present Marshall county was reported to be "one continued train of wagons and cattle," and a traveler frequently had to leave the road "five or six miles to get sufficient grass for his animals." [p. 1104.]

1854, May.—After traveling from Fort Laramie to Independence, Mo., during the latter half of the month the mail party reported that they had encountered "trains of cattle and emigrant parties . . . almost every hour of the day." [p. 1209.]

The above items have been excerpted from another bicentennial commemorative book published by the Kansas State Historical Society in 1972 compiled by staff member Louise Barry under the title *The Beginning of the West, Annals of the Kansas Gateway to the American West, 1540-1854*. The page numbers shown are from this work.

Alcove Spring, discovered by Edwin Bryant half a mile east of the ford across the Big Blue river (present Marshall county) in 1846, was a favorite camping place for wearied travelers on the nearby Oregon trail. Mrs. Sarah Keyes, of the ill-fated Donner party, was buried here May 29, 1846.

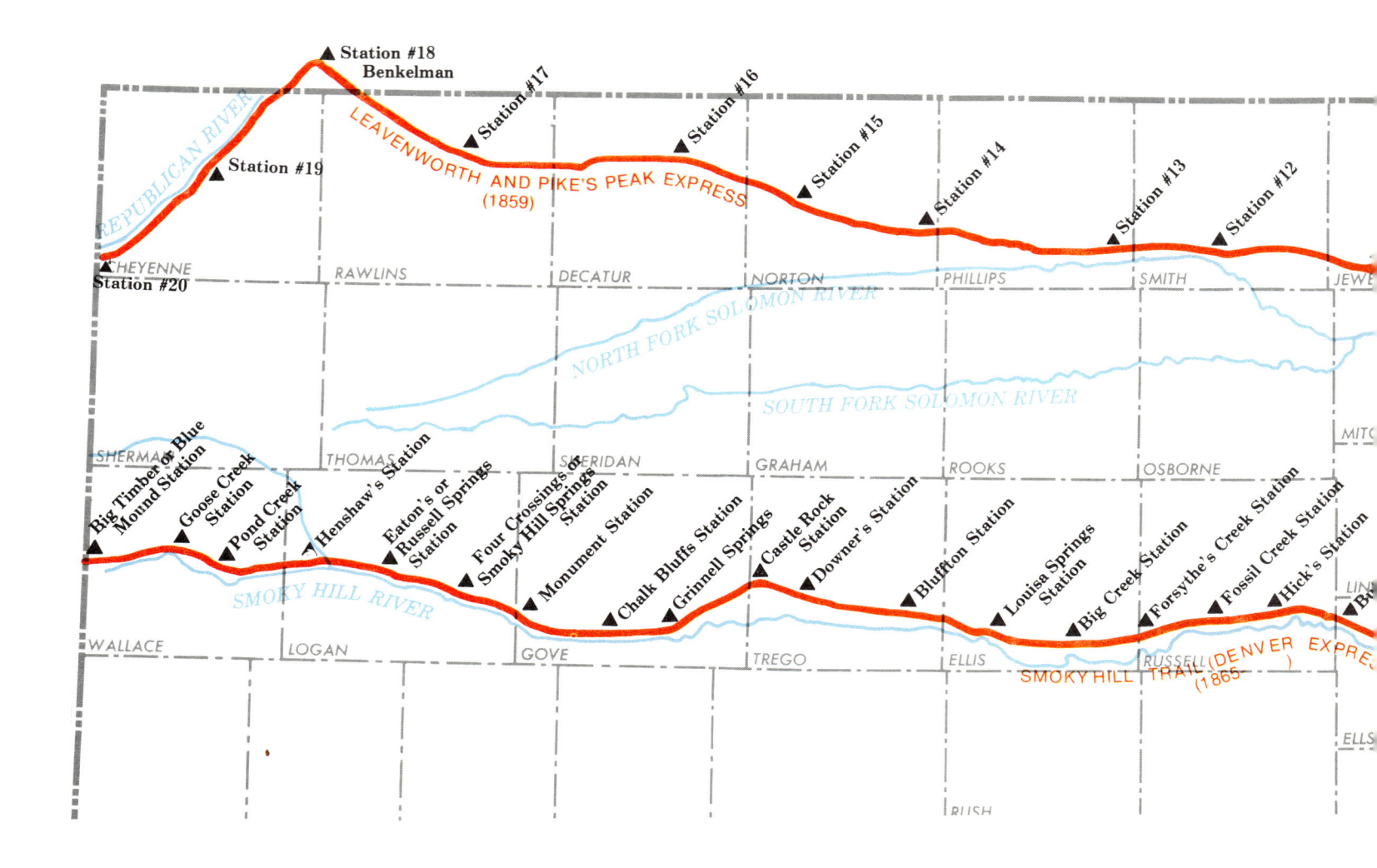

Express and Stage Lines

In April, 1859, the Leavenworth and Pike's Peak Express Company began operating between Leavenworth and the newly discovered gold fields around Denver. The route followed the military road to Fort Riley, then angled northwest and west to the Republican near present Benkelman, Neb., and went up that river until it struck across country once more to reach Denver.

Stations were numbered, not named, and 19 of the 27 lay within the bounds of the state of Kansas (though most of the route was in the then territory of Kansas). At station 10, near present Glasco, author Albert D. Richardson wrote that he and his fellow travelers dined as they sat "upon billets of wood, carpetsacks, and nail-kegs, while the meal was served upon a box. It consisted of fresh buffalo meat, which tastes like ordinary beef though of coarser fiber, and sometimes with a strong, unpleasant flavor. . . . Six weeks ago not a track had been made upon this route. Now it resembles a long-used turnpike. We meet many returning emigrants, who declare the mines a humbug; but pass hundreds of undismayed gold-seekers still pressing on."

Horace Greeley was also a passenger on the coach. At station 15, on Prairie Dog creek in present Norton county, he wrote that "we are now just half way from Leavenworth to Denver, and our coach has been a week making this distance; so that with equal good fortune we may expect to reach the land of gold in another week."

Shortly after the Leavenworth and Pike's Peak Express began, some Atchison residents, through the Atchison and Cherry Creek Bridge and Ferry Company, laid out a new road which cut 65 miles off the route to Denver. Called the Parallel Road because it closely followed the first standard parallel across Kansas, it joined the L.& P.P.E. at station 11 and thereafter followed that line west. An attempt by Atchison to retain some of the remunerative Missouri river traffic to the West, it failed to lure the express coaches off the Solomon and Republican route.

That was accomplished, however, when less than a month after the line was opened Jones, Russell & Company, its owners, purchased a mail contract from John M. Hockaday which necessitated a change of the route from the Solomon and Republican river valleys to that of the Platte. Subsequently, on July 2, 1859, the first stage over this new route left Leavenworth. In February, 1860, the Central Overland California and Pike's Peak Express Company was organized to replace the old Leavenworth and Pike's Peak company. John S. Jones and William H. Russell remained in the new organization and were joined by, among others, Alexander Majors and William B. Waddell.

Shortly after the C.O.C.& P.P.E. was activated, the Pony Express, which offered fast mail service from St. Joseph, Mo., to Sacramento, Calif., was inaugurated. Beginning in April, 1860, the ponies raced through six northeast Kansas counties before entering Nebraska. Over much of its Kansas route, the Pony Express followed the line and used the facilities of the C.O.C.& P.P.E. Each rider was expected to cover at least 33-1/3 miles per run, changing ponies every ten to 15 miles.

At the same time the Pony Express was in operation a transcontinental telegraph line was being built along much of the route the Union Pacific railroad would later take and as the copper wires stretched west the Pony Express was shortened. Finally, after only a year and a half of operation, the Express was discontinued; the wires had reached California.

In 1862 the Central Overland California and Pike's Peak Express, whose initials some said meant "clean out of cash and poor pay," was purchased by Ben Holladay, the stagecoach king, and renamed the Overland Stage Line.

Down along the Smoky Hill river David A. Butterfield established a stage line which he thought could offer stiff competition to the Platte route because of the shorter distance to Denver. Called the Butterfield Overland Despatch, it commenced operation in 1865 but was sold next year to Holladay. That gentleman, perhaps seeing the end of overland staging in Kansas as the Union Pacific, Eastern Division railroad built west, shortly thereafter sold out to Wells, Fargo and Company. Again the stage line grew shorter as the railroad moved toward Denver and in 1870 was no longer needed to connect eastern Kansas with the Colorado Rockies.

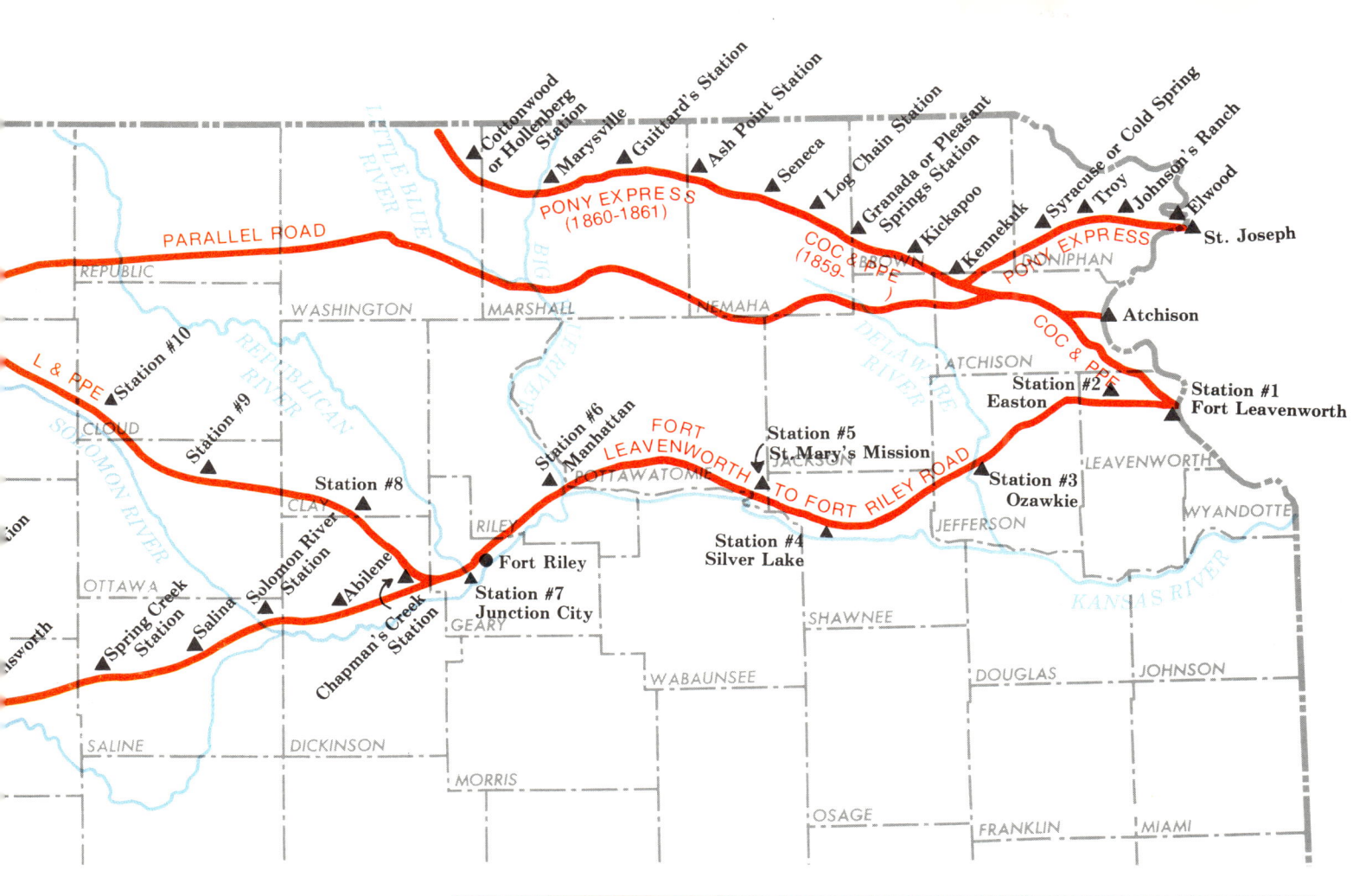

This representation of a stage coach silhouetted by a prairie fire, drawn by Carl Bolmar, illustrated a personal experience of Frank A. Root in 1863 which he described in *The Overland Stage to California,* the book in which the picture was originally published.

Carrying letters and telegraphic dispatches at four dollars each, the Pony Express made weekly trips between St. Joseph, Mo., and Sacramento, Calif., in as little as eight days. Here Bolmar gives his impression of a typical rider.

The 1859 Gold Rush

Traffic over Kansas' famed trails to Santa Fe, or to Oregon and California, was not limited to those who traveled to the Far Places. During the several decades they were in use Nearer Places also attracted emigrants by the thousands. In the late 1850's a gold strike was made in the Pike's Peak region, which was then included in the western part of Kansas territory. This "Western Kansas Gold Strike" brought out hordes of emigrants heading over the trails, each hoping to make his fortune in a hurry.

Dr. M. A. Campdoras, of northern Shawnee county, got the fever, and then had second thoughts. His brother-in-law, Samuel J. Reader, who kept a diary for many years (now preserved by the Kansas State Historical Society), painted Campdoras as he might have appeared "Going to Pike's Peak." Two pages later he painted the doctor "Coming from Pike's Peak," the "way we said he **would** have returned, had he finally gone to seek gold."

Going

Returning

Albert Bierstadt Photographs of 1859

With the Col. Frederick West Lander wagon train starting west from Missouri in May, 1859, over the St. Joseph, Mo.-Marysville route of the Oregon-California trail were several young artists including Albert Bierstadt, who later achieved fame for his magnificent paintings of the American West. The three photographs reproduced below were taken by Bierstadt on this Lander expedition of 1859.

"Pike's Peak Emigrants, St. Joseph, Mo."—This Missouri river city was bustling with gold rush traffic in 1859. Many of these gold seekers would take the Marysville route of the Oregon trail before turning off to the Pike's Peak region.

"Ford of the Little Blue, Kansas."—The Oregon-California trail struck the Little Blue river in northeastern Washington county and followed up that stream (which was "skirted with a thin growth of cottonwood," reported the guidebook).

"Wolf River Ford, Kansas."—The banks of the stream were "very steep and miry," said a guidebook of 1850. The crossing was some five miles from the Presbyterian Iowa, Sac & Fox Mission in Doniphan county. See Bierstadt's facing painting, "Wolf River, Kansas."

ALBERT BIERSTADT'S "WOLF RIVER, KANSAS"

Bierstadt became one of America's greatest painters of Western and mountain scenes. This painting, depicting Wolf river crossing of the Oregon-California trail in Doniphan county, was probably done in the late 1860's. It was derived from the picture "Wolf River Ford, Kansas" (see opposite page) which the artist had photographed in 1859. Painters, like poets, obviously are privileged to indulge in unlimited license. Yet all the ingredients—Indians, white men, tipis, horses and dogs—were in the northeast Kansas area at the time, and the famed photographer-painter merely brought them together in one of his most artistic masterworks of color.

U. S. Forts
and the Years of the Indian Wars

FRONTIER MILITARY POSTS IN KANSAS
(In Chronological Order by Date of Establishment)

Cantonment Martin, 1818-1819

Fort Leavenworth, 1827-

Fort Scott, 1842-1853, 1857-1858, 1861, 1862-1865, 1869-1873

Fort Mann, 1847-1848

Fort Atkinson (Camp Mackay), 1850-1854

Fort Riley (Camp Centre), 1853-

Fort Larned (Camp on Pawnee Fork), 1859-1878

Fort Aubrey (Camp Wynkoop), May, 1864-1866

Fort Harker (Fort Ellsworth), c. August, 1864-1873

Fort Zarah, September, 1864-1869

Fort Dodge, September, 1865-1882

Fort Hays (Fort Fletcher), October 18, 1865-1889

Fort Wallace (Camp Pond Creek), October 26, 1865-1882

George Catlin's portrait of Brig. Gen. Henry Leavenworth (founder of the fort bearing his name), which was painted in miniature at Fort Gibson, Indian territory, in 1834, shortly before the general's death.

The well-used road leading to Fort Leavenworth as sketched by Henry W. Waugh in 1858.

Fort Leavenworth, founded in 1827, is the oldest military post established by the United States west of the Mississippi river still in operation, and remains perhaps the best known of all American forts. Early a cornerstone of this nation's expansion west of the Mississippi, it was engaged in peacekeeping and supply activities during the whole of the Plains Indian wars and the Mexican war of the latter 1840's. The fort was considerably involved in policing territorial Kansas and in the Civil War in the West. Today Fort Leavenworth functions as a Command and General Staff College for American officers and for the nearly 100 who annually come from allied nations the world over.

Post headquarters at Fort Leavenworth in 1872. Over 54 regular army and 43 volunteer regiments have been a part of the fort's history. Many of today's U. S. military leaders and others from associated nations have received training at Fort Leavenworth.

Founded in 1842 and named for Gen. Winfield Scott, Fort Scott was one of several posts established on a line from Minnesota to Louisiana to provide a military buffer zone between settlers and the Indians. Fort Scott is now being rehabilitated and reconstructed in part under the direction of the National Park Service. The officers' quarters, hospital and guardhouse are shown as they look today.

The Indian War Years

Since the first wandering groups of Indian peoples entered what is now Kansas many millennia ago, numerous cultures have come and gone. The total population was never large, probably not more than a few tens of thousands, even after the massive movement of Eastern tribes here in the 19th century. Their camps, hamlets and villages were scattered and the various bands and tribes usually lived together peacefully. However, as their numbers increased and other groups migrated into the plains, raiding would occur for prisoners, trophies and vengeance. Sometimes tribes would ally themselves against a common enemy and then form new alliances. The stronger could and sometimes did drive out or annihilate those who lacked the means or will to defend themselves. Ultimately it was the Europeans and later the new Americans who sought to occupy and hold this land.

From the 1541 visit of Coronado, which was the beginning of recorded history in Kansas, through 1878—the year of the last Indian raid in the state—there never was a time when early explorers, travelers or settlers were not subject to Indian attack. It was inevitable, for no other recourse was available to the Indian except to resist whenever and wherever he felt he had a chance to strike and get away.

The Indian tribes eventually were subdued, as countless other peoples of the world have been, by stronger, more aggressive groups. Though many now protest this seeming injustice on the part of the United States, it nevertheless continues to be the mode of general behavior the world over, even to this day.

In spite of the number of military posts established in Kansas during the first 75 years of the United States' claim to the area (see list of major posts, p. 22), it should not be assumed that the government and Indians were constantly at war. In fact these early posts had several missions, some peaceful, in relation to the Indian. Forts Leavenworth and Scott were established on the then western line of white civilization, ostensibly to protect these on the one side, and the Indians on the other. These forts, later with Fort Riley, began to give protection to travelers using the trails, and with other posts established in the heart of western Kansas Indian lands they also helped to keep peace among the score of Indian tribes. Many forts became bases for distribution of annuities and goods to the Indians as part of this peacekeeping role. All at sometime or other served as supply depots for troops in the field and for posts farther to the west and south.

Fort Riley, first planned as Camp Centre in 1852, was sketched by John Gaddis ten years later. Long a United States cavalry training center, it is now the home of the First infantry division.

Fort Larned, one of the posts located on the Santa Fe trail, was established just west of present Larned in 1859. Though abandoned in 1878 the buildings were well preserved and today constitute the state's only National Historic Site. The sketch above by Ado Hunnius was drawn in 1867 while the photograph at right shows an officers' quarters in 1974.

The frontier army seldom had sufficient force to win a decisive victory against the Indians in Kansas. However, when the Civil War ended, more soldiers became available for a time. In the spring of 1867 an expedition of some 1,400 men, commanded by Maj. Gen. W. S. Hancock, moved toward a Cheyenne camp in the present southern Ness county area, west of Fort Larned. It succeeded in arriving only after the Indians had fled, so the troops burned the camp. This was the first summer on the Kansas plains for Bvt. Maj. Gen. George A. Custer, lieutenant colonel of the Seventh U. S. cavalry, who was in charge of Hancock's mounted troops. When Custer wrote to his wife of the expedition's plans he was certain "the Indians would be so impressed with the magnitude of the expedition that, after the council, they would accept terms and abandon the war-path." Custer, though, was habitually to underestimate the capabilities of the Indian.

As Hancock's expedition neared the Cheyenne camp it suddenly was confronted by a massive array of warriors, ready for battle. As Custer told it:

> The infantry was in the advance, followed closely by the artillery, while my command, the cavalry, was marching on the flank. General Hancock, who was riding with his staff at the head of the column, coming suddenly in view of the wild fantastic battle array, which extended far to our right and left and not more than a half mile in our front, hastily sent orders to the infantry, artillery, and cavalry to form line of battle, evidently determined that if war was intended we should be prepared. The cavalry, being the last to form on the right, came into line on a gallop, and, without waiting to align the ranks carefully, the command was given to "draw saber." As the bright blades flashed from their scabbards into the morning sunlight, and the infantry brought their muskets to carry, a most beautiful and interesting sight was spread out before and around us, presenting a contrast which, to the military eye, could be but striking. Here in battle array, facing each other, were the representatives of civilized and barbarous warfare.... Neither side seemed to comprehend the object or intentions of the other; each was waiting for the other to deliver the first blow. A more beautiful battle-ground could not have been chosen. Not a bush or even the slightest irregularity of ground intervened between the two lines which now stood frowning and facing each other.

It remained for Col. Edward W. Wynkoop, agent to the Cheyenne, to preserve the peace that day. He requested Roman Nose to come forward and talk to Hancock, who asked the war leader directly if he wished to fight. "If we did, we would not come so close to your big guns," was the rejoinder. When the Cheyennes fled that night Custer and the cavalry were dispatched to intercept them, but the Indian trail was lost and they escaped. After other hard and unsuccessful rides on the hot Kansas plains in later pursuits, Custer may have decided that hunting buffalo was much more rewarding than chasing elusive Indians. In 1869 and 1870, his last summers in Kansas, much of his time was devoted to entertaining buffalo-hunting guests in his field camp near Fort Hays. Meanwhile the Indians seemed only to strike when they thought the odds were with them. The much-too-small army stationed in Kansas during the Indian wars seldom could muster more than two or three companies for an emergency since the troops generally were scattered in small squads guarding stage stations and answering Indian alarms over the Plains.

The last Indian raid in Kansas occurred in the autumn of 1878, when Northern Cheyenne chiefs Little Wolf and Dull

An Indian Attack at Walnut Creek

THE DAILY TIMES.

FOR PRESIDENT:
Abraham Lincoln.
FOR VICE-PRESIDENT:
Andrew Johnson.

LEAVENWORTH, KANSAS:
FRIDAY MORNING, JULY 29.

GOLD.
Gold opened yesterday at 151½@152 premium, and closed at 148. Certificates, 94½; 5-20s 108¼.

A GENERAL INDIAN WAR ON THE PLAINS, FAIRLY OPENED!

260 Head of Stock Taken from Ft. Larned!

Two Men Scalped Alive, and Three Others Wounded!

Kiowas, Comanches and Arapahoes Making War in Earnest!

FORT LARNED, July 21.
COL. VAUGHAN:
Since coming to this place, about the first of last June, I have written several letters, among others, one to his Excellency, Thomas Carney, Governor of Kansas, detailing the situation of affairs at this post, and my reasons for believing that several Indian tribes, including the Cheyennes, Kiowas, Comanches and a part of the Arapahoes, had resolved to wage war on the whites. On the morning of the 17th of July, (Sunday) portions of the Apaches, Kiowas and Comanches came to the post, as they had been doing for several days, to get provisions,—over ten thousand dollars worth were issued to them by the commander of the post, within the past few days. Soon after dinner, I, acting officer of the day, was looking for a white boy, said to be a prisoner among them. While I was there, a Kiowa chief, Satank, shot at a sentinel, slightly cutting his arm with an arrow, and gave the signal to run off the stock from the post. I had a fair opportunity of seeing that all the different tribes obeyed the signal. I made my way into the post, not knowing but a shower of arrows would pass through every step that I made.

127 horses belonging to the Colorado battery, 47 Gov't mules, 60 horses and mules belonging to the Sutler and others, the beef herd and some private cattle, were captured by them within a quarter of a mile of the post.

Soon we were completely invested by the Indians. They burned the bridge over Pawnee Fork, distant only a mile and a half. A party was sent, under Lieutenant Eayre, to attack and destroy the Kiowa lodges, not more than three miles distant, but before they had proceeded half way, some five or six hundred Indian warriors took a position to cut them off, while two or three hundred took position in their front. Of course the party had to fall back. Some skirmishing ensued, when darkness closed the operations of the day. On Monday morning, soon after daylight, the Indians appeared on all sides. Yesterday, Wednesday 20th, 4 or 500 appeared again.

On Monday morning of the 18th, a party of about one hundred Indians, principally boys, rode slowly toward a train in front of Capt. O. T. Dunlap's camp, at Walnut Creek, 30 miles East of here. Arriving at the train, they began saluting and shaking hands in a friendly manner. They proceeded to the rear of the train, and began to shoot and murder the teamsters in the most horrible manner. They killed ten men, scalped two alive and wounded three others. Capt. Dunlap, with his company, rushed to the assistance of the train, but soon discovered a large body of Indians, 300 or more, proceeding from the woods of Walnut Creek, with the intention of cutting him off from his fortifications, which compelled him to fall back. He succeeded however, in driving the party from the train, and saving part of the men and stock.

This party of boys were undoubtedly sent to attack the train for the purpose of drawing the troops out, while the braves would cut them off from their fort, and destroy the company. The Arapahoes were engaged in this attack.

The following is a list of the names and residences of those who who were scalped alive, killed and wounded:

SCALPED ALIVE.
Allan W. Edwards, (will probably live), of Kossuth, Desmoines Co., Iowa. Robert Magee, of Easton, Kansas, (will not live). A boy of 13 or 14 years of age.

KILLED AND SCALPED.
William Weddell, Brownsville, Neb. Perry Bealce and son, do. James Lassel, Rob't Lucas, and Lewis Sampson, Clay Co., Mo. Talbot O. Edwards, Desmoines Co., Iowa. Enos Gardner, residence not known. Perry and Charles, negroes from Leavenworth City, killed but not scalped. The killed were buried at Walnut Creek, and those scalped alive are in the hospital at this post; also James Crockman, Wm. Redding and A. M. Gentry, of Brownsville, Neb., wounded.

The savages who committed these outrages were furnished provisions from this post. Whether the commander was deceived by their professions of friendship, or thought to modify their hostility, or acted in obedience to orders from higher authority, I can't say.

The Cheyennes have two white women prisoners. I might write many more things, but my article is becoming longer than I intended. I have given some of the facts. Many more outrages will be heard of soon. I will only add that the morning reports showed only 75 men for duty at this post; Capt. Dunlap's at Walnut Creek, about 60, not more, probably less.
R. M. FISH.

Leavenworth *Daily Times*, July 29, 1864.

How close to the surface lies the past of this relatively new country. When April rains in 1973 caused Walnut creek to flood a few miles east of Great Bend, the water began to expose ten shallowly buried skeletons on the creek bank with metal arrowheads still embedded in some of the bones. Historical Society archeologists were called in, and determined that these were the remains of teamsters killed in 1864 by a large Indian war party. They were part of a wagon train bound from Leavenworth to Fort Union, N. M., on the Santa Fe trail. At the time of the attack they were only about a mile from Camp Dunlap, where 45 men of the 15th Kansas volunteer cavalry were building Fort Zarah. The troopers, fearing an ambush, could offer no assistance but did venture out later to aid the wounded and bury the dead. (At the left is a story of the attack as it appeared in the Leavenworth *Daily Times*.)

Knife, and about 350 of their tribe, broke out of their reservation in what is now Oklahoma in an attempt to return to the Northern Plains. As the band fled across western Kansas from south to north, they killed some 40 Kansas settlers. Troops caught up with them briefly in Scott county when Col. William H. Lewis was killed. Still the army heads simply could not believe what they were hearing and therefore could not get moving fast enough to stop them. At Fort Hays a young West Point graduate, 2Lt. Calvin Cowles, was with troops detailed to intercept the Indians. His feelings were expressed in a letter to his father:

> If we punish the indians we are butchers and murderers and if we fail to do so we are cowards—in the eyes of the people. There is no doubt that these indians were starving and dying of fever and were justified in leaving their reservations. . . . Our sympathies were therefore with them at first but when we reached their trail of murder, rapine and desolation our blood rose against them and there was not a man who would not gladly have risked his life to avenge the defenceless men, women and children who had been so barberously murdered and outraged.

Although this outbreak of 1878 proved to be the last Indian raid in Kansas there were rumors in later years of other impending attacks. In the summer of 1885 a major "scare" in the state's southern border counties caused 15 companies of infantry and ten of cavalry to be assembled at Crisfield in Harper county and in smaller camps elsewhere to scour the area for "hostiles." Since none were found it was suspected that the rumors might have originated with cattlemen who wished to frighten the hordes of settlers arriving that year to engage in widespread breaking up of lands previously available for grazing.

From a careful check of contemporary records it would appear that the following statements might be correct assessments of the Indian-U. S. confrontation in the sweep of Kansas history: Many U. S.-Indian treaties were made and broken, often by both sides when it proved advantageous to do so. Since a greater number of persons had an interest in the government-military-settler side there were more infractions by them than by the Indians. . . . Some of the Eastern Indian tribes removed to Kansas during the 1830's to 1850's had their trails-of-tears similar to those experienced by the five civilized tribes moving into present Oklahoma. . . . Although the white man brought smallpox, cholera and other epidemics with him, they were not given to the Indians deliberately for the whites suffered and died also. There were even earnest efforts in the years when cholera and smallpox were rampant to administer vaccines to the Indians, and many of them responded. . . . In the whole history of Indian-versus-white warfare in what became Kansas, Indians killed more Indians than did the whites and their allies. . . . Quite likely, too, smallpox and cholera killed more whites, and Indians, than did warfare between the races. . . . Almost to a person those pioneering settlers nearest to the Indian and therefore subject to his surprise attacks were the most vehement against him. . . . But it should be said that despite treachery on both sides there was more peace than war between the two groups—with even some touching incidents of helpfulness toward one another.

Fort Dodge was one of a series of posts established at the end of the Civil War along the line of the Santa Fe trail. In 1872 the town of Dodge City was laid out on the west edge of the military reservation. When the post was abandoned the property was turned over to the state and is now a home for ex-soldiers and their families. This scene by Theodore R. Davis, printed in *Harper's Weekly*, depicts the post sutler's store in 1867.

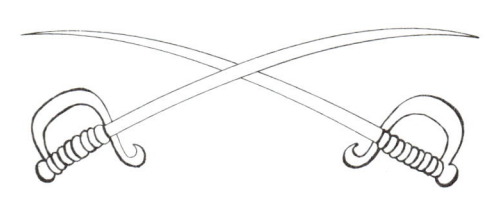

Fort Hays at its first site 14 miles southeast of Hays City. After a flash flood on June 7, 1867, the fort was moved to a more suitable location now just south of the city.

Today the grounds and the few remaining Fort Hays buildings, the blockhouse (above), the guardhouse (at right), and an officers' quarters (not pictured) are the property of the state, administered as a public museum by the State Historical Society.

Satanta, a picturesque chief of the Kiowas, attended the Medicine Lodge peace councils and, though he claimed "I love the land and the buffalo, and will not part with any," signed a treaty which placed his people on a reservation in present Oklahoma.

Treaties at Medicine Lodge, October, 1867

In the fall of 1867, after a summer of bloody skirmishing between Indians and whites, a United States peace commission made up of generals, governors, senators and other high officials met with leaders of the Kiowa, Comanche, Arapaho, Cheyenne and Apache tribes on Medicine Lodge creek in present Barber county to discuss and sign agreements of peace. After several days of parley, the Indians agreed to withdraw their opposition to the construction of railroads on the Smoky Hill and Platte rivers and to military posts which had been established in the West. While reserving the right to hunt south of the Arkansas river, they promised to contain themselves within reservations established by the government. The United States in turn agreed to build storehouses and other buildings; provide seed, clothing and medical care; employ a farmer to teach them to cultivate their soil, a blacksmith to repair their wagons and teachers to educate their children; and to build a mill to grind their corn.

Both Indians and whites, said the reporters from nearly a dozen magazines and newspapers, were well satisfied with the treaties. Henry M. Stanley, who later found Dr. David Livingstone in Africa but then a reporter for the St. Louis *Missouri Democrat*, expressed the feelings of many when he wrote: "Universal malediction light upon the man who will cause the Indian to dig up his hatchet, and all blessings shower upon those who keep the peace." Unfortunately, within eight months both sides were again attacking one another throughout the area of the Great Plains.

"Camp of the Peace Commissioners at Medicine Lodge Creek" and "Satanta Addressing the Peace Commissioners" were the titles given these watercolors by the artist, Hermann Stieffel. Shown in the lower painting are Gens. A. H. Terry, C. C. Augur and W. S. Harney. N. G. Taylor, commissioner of Indian affairs, is probably the civilian seated with them. Private Stieffel was a member of Co. K, Fifth U. S. infantry, detailed as part of the escort for the peace commission. The view of Fort Harker on the following page was also painted by Stieffel.

Fort Harker, like Forts Wallace and Hays, was intended to establish peace on the western Kansas plains. A major quartermaster supply depot for a time, it was active through much of the Indian troubles following the Civil War. Pvt. Hermann Stieffel, who painted this view in watercolors, was stationed at Fort Harker in 1867-1873. It shows the fort's south side, and probably was done about 1870.

The Battle of the Arickaree

In late summer of 1868 a group of nearly 50 Kansas scouts commanded by Bvt. Col. George A. Forsyth was sent from Fort Wallace to find Indians who had attacked a civilian wagon train and the town of Sheridan, a dozen miles to the east. In northeastern Colorado they came upon several hundred Cheyenne and Sioux warriors who attacked and surrounded them on a sandy island in the nearly dry Arickaree river. For several days, during which three men were killed and 18 wounded, they beat off repeated Indian attacks while their food supply dwindled until they were reduced to eating prickly pears, cactus, coyote and decayed horse meat. The Indians suffered higher casualties, including the loss of their war leader, Roman Nose.

Forsythe made several attempts to send men for help. Some disappeared into the night but others came back, unable to get through the Indian lines. Though the attacks had ceased by the fourth day, the exhausted men and wounded on the island were in constant fear of renewed fighting. Scout Chauncey B. Whitney, later to be murdered as sheriff of Ellsworth county, wrote in his diary on September 24: "My God have you deserted us?" The next day, however, he recorded "a day long to be remembered by our little band of Heros." Four of the scouts had made it through the lines and the first help, in the form of units of the 10th United States cavalry, arrived at last. In combat or not, regulation pay for these heroic Kansas scouts was about two dollars per day.

"The Battle of the Arickaree (or Beecher Island)," painted by Robert Lindneux in 1926.

General Custer and his wife Libbie, with brother Cpt. Tom Custer, at ease on the little gallery which extended to the rear of the Custer tent on Big creek, not far from Fort Hays, in the summer of 1869. The general and Tom were killed in the Battle of the Little Big Horn in Montana on June 25, 1876.

Two British lords (to the left of tent opening)—Waterpark in chair, Paget on ground—with others who were part of a buffalo-hunting party of over 200 persons, conducted to what is now Rush county in early September, 1869, by Bvt. Maj. Gen. George A. Custer (lying on the ground at the left), under escort of 100 picked troopers. The safari departed from Fort Hays with colors flying and its band playing "God Save the Queen" in compliment to the titled English guests. Forty buffalo were brought down in the first day's hunt. But not all army officers killed buffalo for sport. Gen. John Pope visited Fort Hays on an inspection trip in 1870 and was heard to "administer a scathing rebuke on the cruelty of those who killed buffalo."

Cheyenne Indians challenge Kansas Pacific railroad track workers west of present Russell on May 28, 1869. Painted in oil in 1931 by Jacob Gogolin.

The Struggle for Statehood and the Civil War

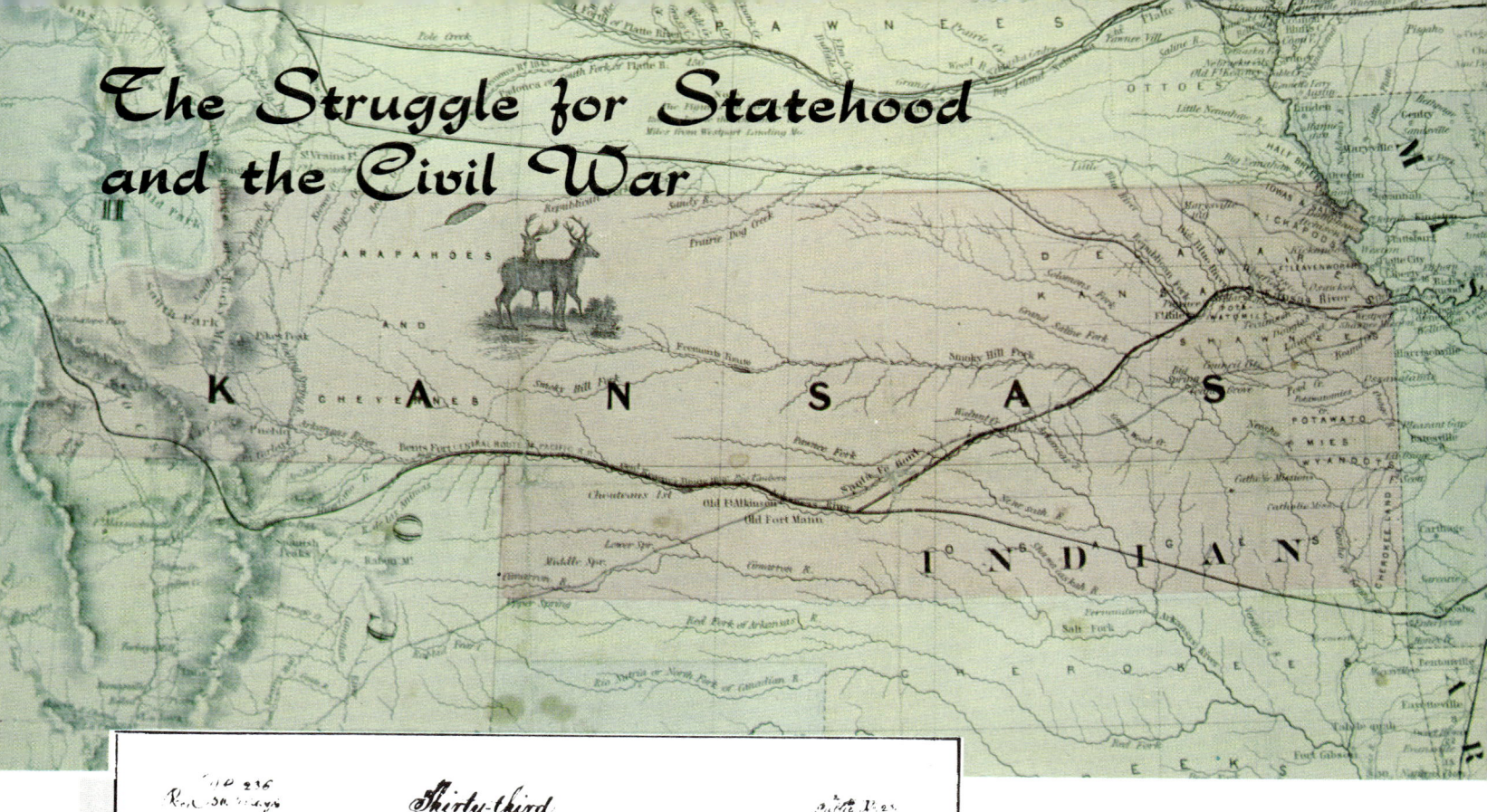

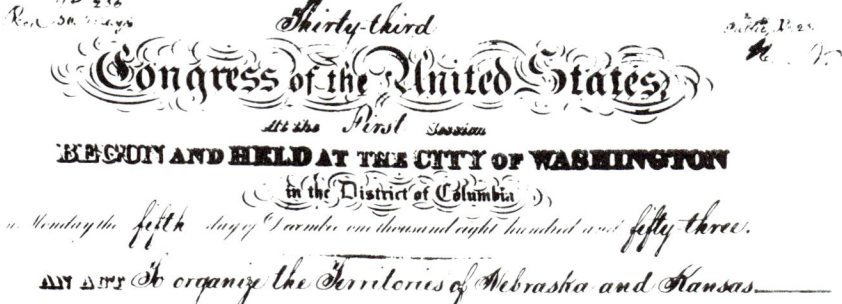

Kansas and Nebraska territories were organized by the Kansas-Nebraska act passed by congress and signed by Pres. Franklin Pierce on May 30, 1854. The boundaries of Kansas were established on the east at the Missouri line, on the west at the crest of the Rockies, on the north at the 40th parallel, and on the south—except for the southwest portion which was then part of New Mexico territory—at the 37th parallel. The act provided for popular sovereignty: voters were to decide for themselves whether Kansas would enter the Union as a free or slave state. Controversy flared almost immediately between Free-State and Proslavery partisans as they poured in to take up land claims. Outspoken editors and fiery politicians debated and declaimed, while fanatical leaders on both sides reacted with violence even including arson and murder. Some observers called these "Bleeding Kansas" difficulties the prelude to the Civil War.

The first page of the "act to organize the territories of Nebraska and Kansas."

Many votes in the first Kansas elections were cast illegally by Proslavery Missourians who hoped to protect their interests by making Kansas a slave state. As a result the out-numbered Free-Staters had little success at the polls. This roistering group shown debarking from a ferry was sketched for an article in *Century* magazine in 1887.

Andrew H. Reeder was a Pennsylvania Democrat who sided with the Free-State cause after he took office as the first territorial governor. He then was scorned by Proslaveryites and was forced to flee Kansas in disguise.

The first territorial legislature, called to meet by Governor Reeder in July, 1855, was almost solidly Proslavery. The legislature met in this building at the infant town of Pawnee, now on the Fort Riley reservation, before adjourning to the more civilized environs of Shawnee Methodist Mission. Known today as the First Territorial Capitol, the building is operated as a museum by the State Historical Society.

James H. Lane, the "Grim Chieftain," represented the radical arm of the Free-State party and believed in violent retaliation against Proslaveryites. Lane later served as one of the state's first U. S. senators until his suicide in 1866.

In May, 1856, the Proslavery sheriff of Douglas county, Samuel Jones, bent on destruction, led a posse into Lawrence, the major Free-State stronghold. The chief damage was the burning of the Free-State Hotel, shown here in a painting by Robert O. Gibbons.

Charles Robinson, elected governor of the short-lived Free-State organization which defied the federally approved government, became the first governor of the state of Kansas in 1861.

Sara T. D. Robinson, wife of Governor Robinson, was also a strong Free-State advocate. She was the author of a book on the territorial days, *Kansas, Its Interior and Exterior Life*.

31

The Kansas territorial controversy over slavery shook the nation when Proslavery forces arrested several Free-State leaders, including Robinson (center), charged them with treason, and imprisoned them for a time at Lecompton. The prisoners are shown here as sketched in *Frank Leslie's Illustrated Newspaper*, New York, October 4, 1856.

In 1855 the celebrated abolitionist John Brown came to Kansas, where he played a violent role in the anti-slavery cause for several months. He is pictured (far right) as he looked at the time of his arrival. The watercolor (right) by Samuel J. Reader, a territorial pioneer and amateur artist, shows Brown on his way to a Free-State camp in 1856.

John Brown

During Brown's first year in Kansas he headed a little band of Free-Staters who murdered five Proslaveryites on Pottawatomie creek in Franklin county.

The cavalry engagement at the battle of Hickory Point in Jefferson county on September 13, 1856, as recorded in watercolors by Samuel J. Reader. Casualties of the two-day fight included one killed and nine wounded.

A Sharps carbine

Among the organized groups which came to help establish a free state was the Connecticut Kansas colony which founded the community of Wabaunsee. They organized the "Beecher Bible and Rifle Church" in 1857 and completed this building in 1862. The name was given to the congregation because Henry Ward Beecher and other Eastern abolitionists contributed Sharps carbines to the colony.

As a kind of last gasp effort by Proslaveryites, Dr. John Doy of Lawrence was kidnapped and tried in Missouri for stealing slaves. While being held in the St. Joseph jail he was freed by friends from Kansas. Doy and his rescuers had their picture taken following the incident (above). The final bloody event of the territorial struggle was the Marais des Cygnes massacre in Linn county (portrayed below). In May, 1858 Missourians murdered five Free-State men. Site of the massacre is now a memorial state park.

Constitution Hall in Lecompton, now a National Historic Landmark, housed a constitutional convention in 1857 which produced a document favoring slavery. It was submitted to congress for approval after its adoption at an election in which no Free-State voters participated and its rejection at an election in which few Proslavers voted. Ultimately it was turned down by congress and Kansas was to wait another two and a half years for statehood.

Statehood Achieved

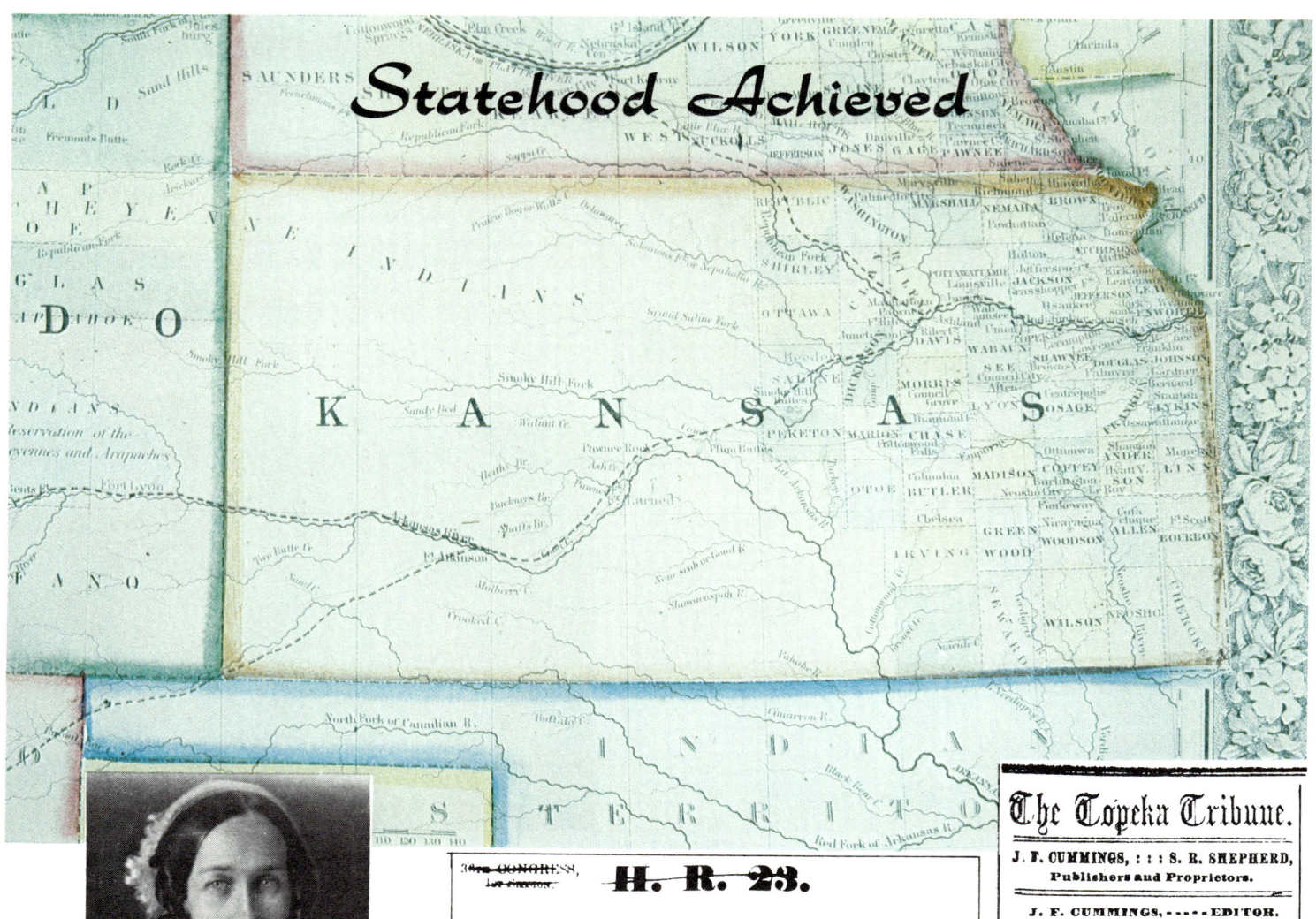

Clarina I. H. Nichols

The unsettled political situation moved toward solution with the adoption of the Wyandotte constitution by Kansas voters in 1859 and the admission of Kansas as a state on January 29, 1861 (see first page of the official copy of the bill, right). At home most Kansans greeted admission with unbounded joy, as indicated in the portion of the account excerpted from a Topeka newspaper (far right). Others, however, including Clarina I. H. Nichols (above), who fought to have more rights for women written into the constitution, were less pleased. Modern Kansans also generally regret the elimination of the portion of the Colorado Rockies which had been included in the Kansas territorial boundaries of 1854-1861. (Compare state map above with territorial map on page 30.)

36TH CONGRESS,
1st Session.

H. R. 23.

[Report No. 266.]

IN THE HOUSE OF REPRESENTATIVES.

FEBRUARY 15, 1860.

Read twice, and referred to the Committee on Territories.

MARCH 29, 1860.

Reported back by Mr. Grow without amendment, and ordered to be printed.

Public 6.

Mr. Grow, on leave, introduced the following bill:

An Act

For the admission of Kansas into the Union.

Whereas the people of the Territory of Kansas, by their representatives in convention assembled, at Wyandott, in said Territory, on the twenty-ninth day of July, one thousand eight hundred and fifty-nine, did form for themselves a constitution and State government, republican in form, which was ratified and adopted by the people at an election held for that purpose, on Tuesday, the fourth day of October, one thousand eight hundred and fifty-nine, and the said convention has, in their name and behalf, asked the Congress of the United States to admit the said Territory into the Union as a State, on an equal footing with the other States: Therefore—

Be it enacted by the Senate and House of Representatives of the United States of America in Congress assembled, That the State of Kansas shall be, and is hereby declared to

---

The Topeka Tribune.

J. F. CUMMINGS, : : : S. R. SHEPHERD,
Publishers and Proprietors.

J. F. CUMMINGS, ——— EDITOR.

TOPEKA, KANSAS.

SATURDAY MORNING, FEB. 2, 1861.

THE STATE OF KANSAS!

"ALL HAIL THOU GLORIOUS ORB!!"

LET THE OLD CANNON SPEAK.

Do Ra Me Fa Sol La Si Do!!!

THE KANSAS BILL

Passed the Senate----Ditto House!

Signed by the President!

LET US ALL REJOICE!!

There is no longer any doubts to be entertained with regard to our admission. The nail is clinched. Kansas is to-day a Sovereign State of the American Union. The following dispatch received by the Leavenworth *Conservative* confirms our anticipations:

WASHINGTON, Jan. 30.
The Kansas Bill has received the President's signature. Mr. Conway appeared on the floor of the House and was sworn in.

At last, our prayer has been answer-

INDEPENDENT KANSAS Jay-Hawkers.

Volunteers are wanted for the 1st Regiment of Kansas Volunteer Cavalry to serve our country

During the War.

Horses will be furnished by the Government. Good horses will be purchased of the owner who volunteers. Each man will be mounted, and armed with a Sharp's Rifle, a Navy Revolver, and a Sabre. The pay will be that of the regular volunteer.

Volunteers from Northern Kansas will rendezvous at Leavenworth. Those from Southern Kansas will rendezvous at Mound City. Volunteers singly, parts of companies and full companies will be mustered into the United States service as soon as they report themselves to the local recruiting officer at either of the above places. Upon arriving at Mound City volunteers will report themselves to John T. Snoddy, Acting Adjutant. Those who rendezvous at Leavenworth will report themselves to D. R. Anthony, Esq. of that place.

C. R. JENNISON,
Col. 1st Regiment Kansas Vol. Cavalry.
MOUND CITY, Aug. 24, 1861.

The Civil War

Kansans in record numbers volunteered for military service after war broke out in the spring of 1861. By the time the South surrendered, four years later, two-thirds of all the adult males in Kansas had seen some kind of duty. The state formed 23 regiments and four artillery batteries for federal service and her units included white, black and Indian troops. They served in Kansas, the Indian territory, and in several Southern states from the Missouri border to Chickamauga. On the home front women and children kept farms and businesses going while fathers and older sons were under arms. Kansans were wholeheartedly behind the Union cause and despite local party differences and some political infighting they made solid contributions to the war effort.

Recruiting poster for the First Kansas cavalry regiment which later became the Seventh Kansas. This unit gained notoriety for its raids in western Missouri but also saw action in Mississippi and Tennessee.

Kansas units at the Battle of Wilson's Creek near Springfield, Mo., August 10, 1861. This action, the first combat for any of the Kansas volunteers, was a defeat for the Union although its outnumbered forces fought bravely.

Below, an all-black field artillery battery at Fort Leavenworth about 1864.

On August 21, 1863, Lawrence was sacked by Confederate guerrillas led by William C. Quantrill. The raid has been described as one of the most despicable acts of the Civil War. Nearly 150 Lawrence men were killed and the town was almost totally devastated. These contemporary drawings show the town aflame and its citizens under attack. (Upper sketch from *Leslie's Illustrated Newspaper,* September 12, 1863; right, as drawn by Mrs. L. L. Fox-Fisk.)

In the fall of 1864 a Confederate force under Maj. Gen. Sterling Price moved west across Missouri, threatening Kansas City and Fort Leavenworth. The Kansas militia was called up to supplement federal troops and fighting took place at several points in the Kansas City area. Shown at the left is the Battle of the Big Blue, October 22, 1864, as later sketched by Samuel J. Reader, one of the Kansas militiamen.

During Price's retreat south along the Kansas-Missouri border he was overtaken on October 25, 1864, at Mine creek in Linn county by pursuing Union forces. Some 10,000 troops were involved in this brief battle at the crossing, making it the largest engagement on Kansas soil during the war. Here many of Price's men were captured and with the remnants of his army he hastened his retreat into Arkansas. The war in the West was over.

During the height of invasion fears, Topekans built a stockade—which came to be known as Fort Simple—in the intersection of Sixth and Kansas avenues as a defense against Price's forces should they penetrate this far west. Years after it was torn down, Topeka artist Henry Worrall painted it in watercolor.

These were some of the men from Kansas who fought the war. There are no high ranking officers in these groups. They are plain foot soldiers, the GI's of any war—farmers, clerks, teachers, and craftsmen, engaged in a common cause.

37

"First Furrow," by O. C. Seltzer, illustrates the confrontation of the old and the new: Indians watching a white settler breaking the prairie sod, an indication of what was to come.

Settlement and Town Building

Although numbers of the earliest settlers in Kansas territory were desirous of creating a Free or Proslavery state, depending on the soundness of each "on the goose,"* nearly everyone had the primary concern of taking up his own agricultural land or investing in town lots and becoming materially successful as quickly as possible. They dreamed big dreams. Nearly all these settlers were poor, but preemption laws (and in 1862 the Homestead act) provided relatively easy and inexpensive ways of becoming landowners. Town companies blossomed overnight, some to prosper and develop into thriving communities but many more to wither as quickly as they bloomed.

The earliest shelters, of course, were constructed from locally available materials. In Lawrence, even some prairie grass was used as a temporary material in the first Emigrant "hotel." Most early eastern Kansas homes, however, were built almost entirely of logs. As the number of sawmills increased lumber for more sophisticated construction became available. Where there was suitable stone, and masons to fashion it, houses of this material began to appear, some remaining to this day. Clay suitable for making bricks was also found in many areas, and local brickyards developed.

As the line of settlement moved west and out of the wooded areas, pioneers made their first homes in dugouts which they carved into hill sides, or they cut tough virgin sod into pieces and laid it up like brick. These soddies required few commercial materials in their construction, were cool in summer and warm in winter, and served efficiently as inexpensive housing.

As the land was gradually tamed and began to yield more than a subsistence living, the residents of the state both rural and urban were able to enjoy the fruits of their labors. Daily life became a little less severe and a few amenities were evidenced in more elaborate homes with interiors sometimes approaching the luxurious. By the end of the century, to paraphrase William Allen White, Kansans had established themselves and the institutions of a strong and viable state by "hard work and pluck" which he called the bases of the Kansas character.

---

*In 1855 Kansas if one were sound on the goose he was ardently Proslavery.—D. W. Wilder, *The Annals of Kansas* (Topeka, 1886), pp. 58, 62.

A primitive log cabin—owner, location and date unknown—evidence of the simplicity of frontier life.

Cabin near Humboldt, Allen county, complete with outdoor kitchen—or soap kettle?

The John Link family and their solidly built cabin in Marshall county, about 1898.

Armed pioneers near Lawrence, 1856.

Buffalo hunters' dugout at Sheridan, about 1874.

Combination dugout-soddy about 1895, probably in Norton county.

A tar paper claim shack in Clay county, easily erected and as easily knocked down but adequate for its temporary purpose.

The Conn homestead in Thomas county, about 1890.

The substantial soddy below, at Beeler, Ness county, in the 1880's and the smaller one (right) at Dighton, Lane county, were hotels, the latter said to be the first in the town.

Jacob Smith family and their soddy in 1884.

Lawrence

Topeka

St. George

Manhattan

Photographs taken along the Kansas (now the Union) Pacific railroad by R. Benecke of St. Louis who made his tour in the mid-1870's. From top to bottom: "General View of Lawrence," "Hotel and Railway station . . . (North) Topeka," "Quail Shooting at St. George," and "Manhattan, . . . From the Summit of Mount Prospect."

Brookville

Ellsworth

Wilson

Bunker Hill

The Benecke photographs reproduced here on both pages, and elsewhere in this book, are used by permission of the owner of the originals, The DeGolyer Foundation Library of Dallas, Tex. Again reading from the top down: "Brookville, Kansas," "Stock Yards and Chutes for Loading Cattle at Ellsworth," "Wilson," and "Bunker Hill."

Almena, Norton county, about 1889.

Below: Other Benecke photographs—taken in the mid-1870's—of Russell, and of the main street of Ellis.

Russell

Ellis

Early views of Kansas towns include (from top to bottom) Haven, Reno county, in 1886; Oakley, Logan county, in 1903, and Empire City, Cherokee county, date unknown.

Mule-drawn wagons line the streets of busy Paola in the 1860's, a decade after the town was born.

Mullinville's main street, open as the land around it, photographed shortly after the town was founded in the mid-1880's.

A four-burro hitch wagon pictured in Liberal at the turn of the century.

Town shares usually worth several lots each—to be selected later through drawings—were sold by company promoters to prospective residents and speculators. Several of these original shares are pictured on the facing page. ▶

SAINT GEORGE TOWN COMPANY.
Kansas Territory.
MARMATON TOWN COMPANY.
Lexington Town Company
JOHNSON COUNTY
KANSAS TERR.
FALLS CITY TOWN ASSOCIATION.
DELAWARE TOWN COMPANY
OF LAWRENCE.
SOUTH TECUMSEH TOWN ASSOCIATION
Nashville.
NASHVILLE TOWN CO.
Nashville, Kansas,
KANSAS LOCATING ASSOCIATION.
PRAIRIE CITY,
Prairie City, Kansas.
CERTIFICATE OF STOCK
MEADE + CENTER + TOWN + COMPANY
POTTOWATOMIE CITY.
Battle Hill.
BATTLE HILL TOWN ASSOCIATION.
Battle Hill, Kansas,
ST. CHARLES.
TOWN OF ST. CHARLES,
THE BLOOMINGTON COMPANY
TOWN OF BLOOMINGTON,
DE SOTO TOWN COMPANY.

"Home Sweet Home"...

TO THIS DETERMINED GROUP was the Anderson sodhouse in Logan county. The "orchestra," because of the gun, may have been ready to play Tchaikovsky's "1812 Overture," perhaps? . . . Or maybe the rifle was to ward off possible objectors to their brand of country music? . . . Oh well, don't fault us for trying.

TO THIS FAMILY OF THE 1880's somewhere in Kansas, was everyone at work but father.

TO THE PROUD OWNER of this outlay who, as often was the custom, posed his family in the window and on the porches, with other prized possessions arranged out front. The photograph, by F. A. Wesely, probably was taken in the early 1900's either in the Holyrood or Wichita areas.

The Stephen H. Fairfield residence at 1108 Throop street in Topeka was typical of middle class America after the turn of the century. Though not rich, the family could afford a servant who was maid, cook and friend. All five of the Fairfield children were graduated from college and life in general was kind. Music and good food were expressive of the gentle life, as these pictures illustrate.

As better construction materials became available Kansans were able to build homes suitable to their needs, tastes and economic status. They ranged from the extremely simple to ornate mansions. Even the lowliest was far superior to the homes of the first settlers. Illustrated on this page (top to bottom) are homes in Butler, Logan and Marshall counties. Notice how tree sizes indicate the age of the house and that in all cases the entire family posed before its home as if to say "this is mine."

Interiors of homes are indicators of family personalities. Even poverty cannot conceal one's desire for order and comfort. The interior of the Ford county dugout (top) appears untidy at first glance, but closer inspection shows that the lady of the house made excellent use of the little space she had. Similarly, the Russell county living room (center) shows that this more settled homemaker appreciated quality and comfort, while the Topeka dining room (bottom) reflects the opulent life style of its owners.

These were typical scenes at the turn of the century—Monday washday with galvanized tubs and corrugated scrub boards, scrubbing with hand brush and broom in Manhattan, little sister feeding the chickens, and neighbors joining forces for the fall hog butchering. Opposite page, wood cutters in Ellsworth county, carpenters adding an ell to a farm home, and finally, a more than usually elaborate dinner in Cheney.

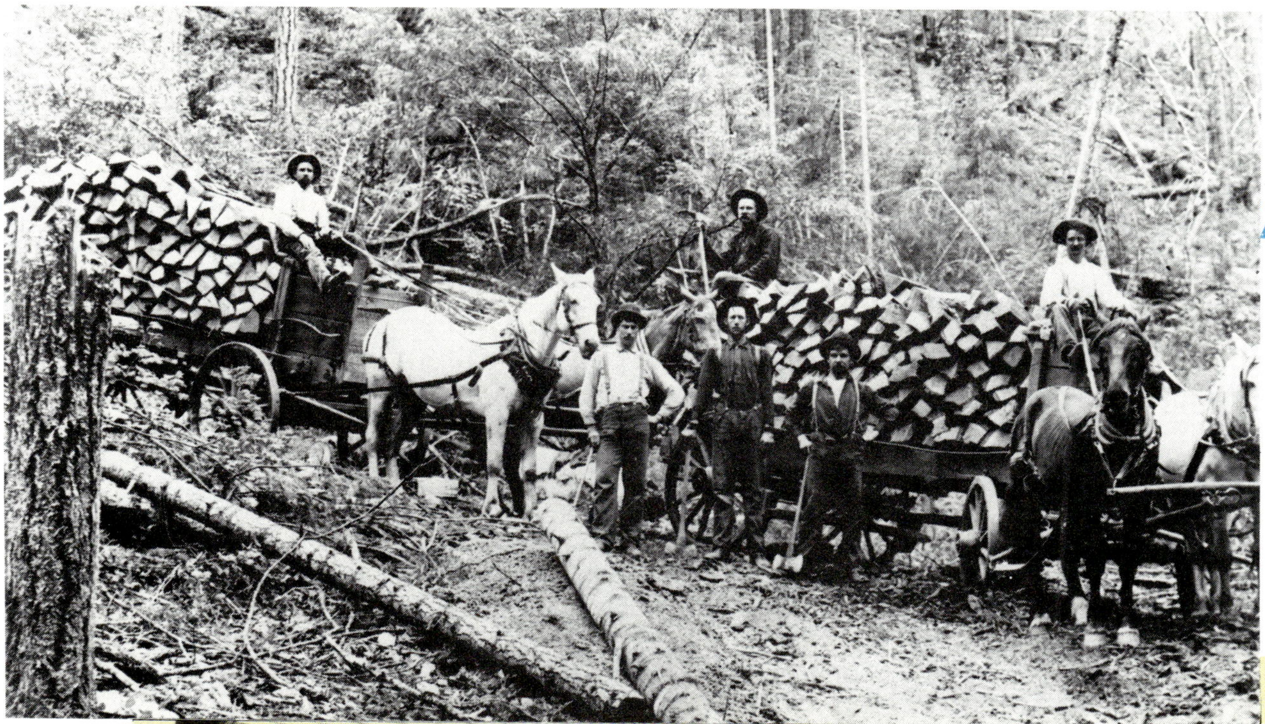

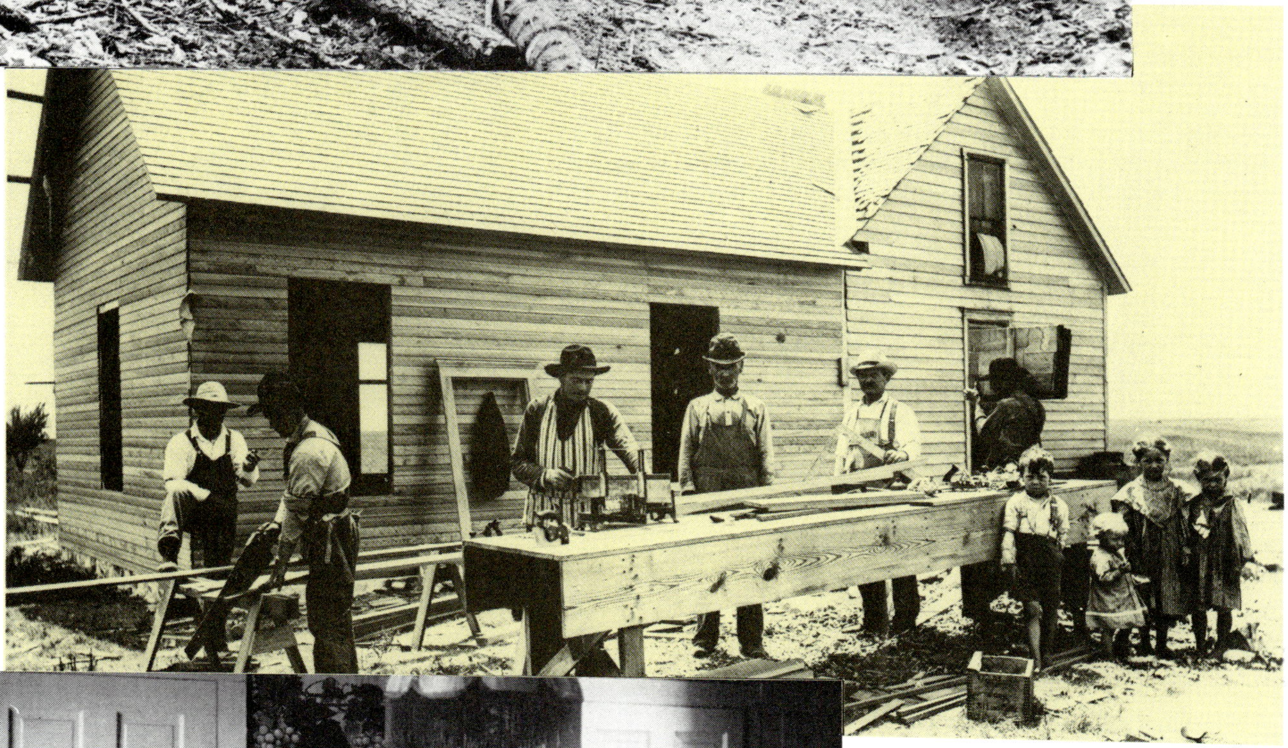

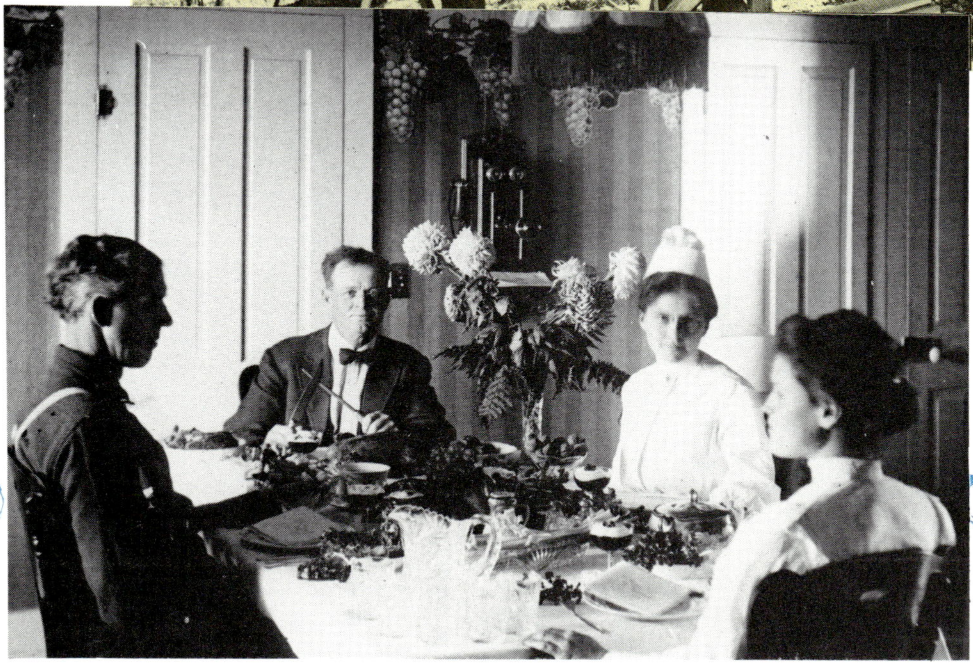

Movement from one place to another has always been a limiting factor in human development. During the eons in which man had to depend on his own two legs his travel was relatively restricted and extensive migration required long periods of time. Eventually he captured and trained animals to carry him and his possessions, and still later developed machines for the same purpose, providing ever better trails and roadways over which they could pass. The pictures on this and the following pages, from the "Knight of the Open Road" (right), who traveled by any means available, to modern machines of the land and the sky, are intended to portray the development of transportation devices.

For several decades, notably in the late 1850's and 1860's, steamboats plied the Missouri river supplying its towns and unloading travelers and freight headed for the Western interior. Several northeast Kansas counties bordered the Missouri river at an advantageous bend, and Kansas profited enormously from this trade. The boats occasionally traveled the Kansas river even as far inland as Manhattan, but often low water stranded them on sandbars. The steamboat *Hartford*, in 1855, was stuck so long near St. Marys that its captain eventually bought a cow, which he tethered on the bank, to provide fresh milk for the crew.

Countless pack-trains, wagon-trains and stagecoaches were involved in Kansas land travel until railroads began crisscrossing the state. Steam, electric and gasoline in-

Getting around in Kansas

Before the days of the railroad, steamboats carried heavy freight and passengers to Kansas' shores. Beginning about 1840 more than 700 craft plied the waters of the Missouri river, many of them serving Kansas river ports. Shown here is the steamer *Mary McDonald* at Wyandotte in 1867. On June 12, 1873, this splendid side-wheeler burned near Waverly, Mo., while lying off shore. Though steamboats were tried on both the Kansas and the Arkansas rivers, shifting sandbars made their runs difficult and uneconomical.

Persons wishing to cross Kansas streams in the early days could either wade or look for a ferry. Before the Kansas river was bridged in the 1860's ferries were found every few miles. The one shown here, though unidentified, is typical of those on the Kaw.

terurbans eventually replaced local stage lines, while street railways and buses provided intracity transportation until declining revenue forced the abandonment of much of this service.

Being in the center of what became known as the contiguous 48 states, Kansas received her share of the major railroads, including the Union Pacific, Santa Fe, Rock Island and Missouri Pacific. By 1888 there were more than 9,250 miles of railroad track in Kansas and in 1892 Kansas ranked third among the states in trackage.

With the development of the automobile and the airplane, railroads began to decline in importance. By 1976 rail passenger service was almost nonexistent, but rail freight service was available to many cities and towns. Highways, at first merely graded dirt roads, later were paved and widened to four and sometimes six lanes, to accommodate the thousands of private automobiles and trucks. Only the larger cities enjoyed commercial air service, but most towns of size boasted an airfield where passenger transportation to national or international airports could be obtained. Fleet buses provide degrees of passenger service across the state and nation, but public passenger transportation is not presently available within and between many Kansas cities and towns. Without doubt, though, it was the people through their patronage—or the lack of it—who determined the courses of these many changes. The fact that in 1974 there were 1,251,826 automobiles to serve the needs of 2,299,220 citizens was clear indication that many Kansans prefer to use their own autos for much of their transportation.

In Kansas, where the wind seems to blow much of the time, it was natural that inventive citizens would occasionally attempt to harness that power to propel wagons. Newspapers record such attempts from the territorial period and it was even said that a successful trip was made all the way to Denver. The wind wagon shown here was a later variety built in Logan county, probably in the 1880's, by George Bull and Clint McIntosh, who proudly pose on its stern.

Stagecoaches, whether military ambulances, Concords or mud wagons, provided both cross country and local passenger and light freight service. As railroads spanned Kansas the long distance stage lines ceased operations but short haul feeder lines existed well into the 20th century. P. G. Reynolds, of Dodge City, was a typical stage line owner. At the top, three of his Dodge City to Ashland coaches are shown at Appleton, a now extinct town in Clark county, in the late 1880's. Below, stagecoaches at a barn in Wellington in the 1890's.

A Carl Bolmar drawing showing a coach of the Leavenworth and Pike's Peak Express in 1859 dashing into Indianola, a once thriving town of Shawnee county now extinct (see page 18).

FOR PIKE'S PEAK, HO!

DAILY U.S. MAIL LINE

Through to Denver City in 6 1-2 Days!

THE CENTRAL OVERLAND, CALIFORNIA

AND

PIKE'S PEAK EXPRESS CO.

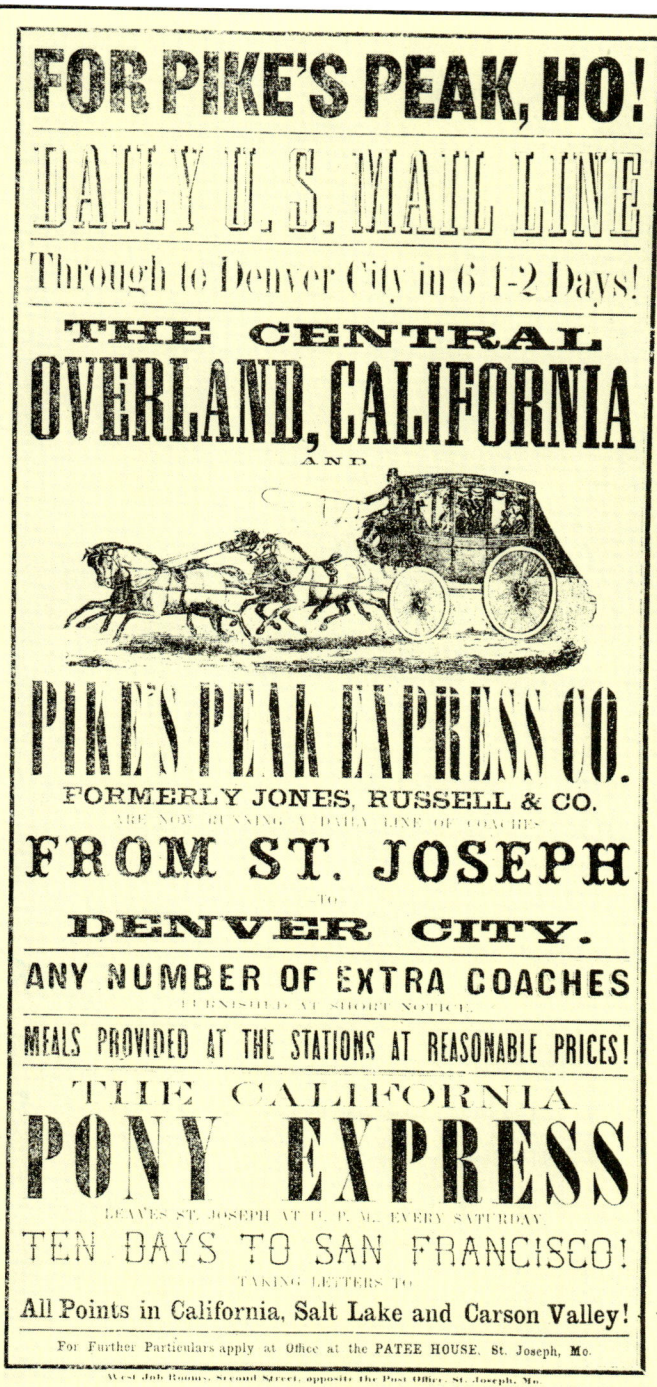

FORMERLY JONES, RUSSELL & CO.

ARE NOW RUNNING A DAILY LINE OF COACHES

FROM ST. JOSEPH

To

DENVER CITY.

ANY NUMBER OF EXTRA COACHES

FURNISHED AT SHORT NOTICE.

MEALS PROVIDED AT THE STATIONS AT REASONABLE PRICES!

THE CALIFORNIA PONY EXPRESS

LEAVES ST. JOSEPH AT 11 P. M. EVERY SATURDAY

TEN DAYS TO SAN FRANCISCO!

TAKING LETTERS TO

All Points in California, Salt Lake and Carson Valley!

For Further Particulars apply at Office at the PATEE HOUSE, St. Joseph, Mo.

West Job Rooms, Second Street, opposite the Post Office, St. Joseph, Mo.

Members of the Dodge City Bicycle Club pose with their ordinaries and tricycles about 1892. At far left is Dr. T. L. McCarty, famed early Dodge City physician.

The first Rural Free Delivery service began in Kansas on October 26, 1896. Though experimental at first, by the turn of the century it was firmly established. This carrier out of Maple Hill in 1899 probably earned the standard $25 a month for delivering packages, letters and telephone and telegraph messages as well.

Kansas immigrants who could not afford steamship or railroad fares often traveled in covered wagons. Few were of the celebrated Conestoga type; most were simple box wagons fitted with bows and covered with canvas. Sometimes household goods were shipped by train while the family traveled in a wagon, but more often everything was carried with them. On arriving at the claim, the new owners occasionally used the wagon as "home" until some sort of semi-permanent shelter could be erected. Shown above is a typical wagon in Greenwood county, date unknown, and, left, the Pearson family in Johnson county, 1908.

Though Kansas climate is not particularly conducive to continued winter sleighing, those vehicles were used when snow cover permitted. This rig was photographed in Sedgwick county.

Inventive Kansans hitched most any kind of creature to most any kind of vehicle. Children used turkeys to pull their wagon in Nortonville.

A huge cask mounted on wheels paraded the streets of Wakefield on a Fourth of July in the 1880's while (below) tired donkeys pulled the spring wagon of this couple in Bonner Springs.

The Arrival of the Iron Horse

A railroad survey crew (above) probably employed by the Union Pacific, Eastern Division, sits for a picture in western Kansas in 1867. Black troops from Co. 1, 38th United States infantry, detailed as guards, pose at left, with teamsters and cooks at right.

Alexander Gardner, an associate of Matthew Brady, who may have taken the survey crew picture, photographed this track laying activity of the UPED (above) 20 miles west of Hays in October, 1867.

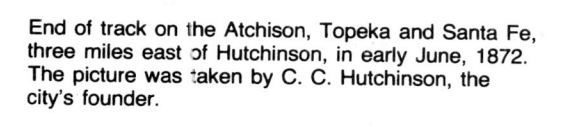

End of track on the Atchison, Topeka and Santa Fe, three miles east of Hutchinson, in early June, 1872. The picture was taken by C. C. Hutchinson, the city's founder.

Section hands followed early construction of Kansas' railroads to straighten and ballast the line, then spent their time maintaining the roadbed. This crew, near Atchison on the Santa Fe line, appears to be replacing ties.

Many Kansas towns owe their establishment and existence to the railroad. Horton, on the line of the Chicago, Kansas and Nebraska (later the Chicago, Rock Island and Pacific) was one. The photo on the right depicts a railroad-promoted sale of town lots in the mid-1880's.

Anthony citizens turned out for the celebration which signaled the beginning of construction on the Kansas City, Mexico and Orient, May 10, 1902. The line, which was proposed to connect Kansas City with Topolobampo, a seaport on the Gulf of California, never reached its goal. In 1929 the northern segment was purchased by the Santa Fe and the southern was taken over by the government of Mexico, which eventually completed it as the Chihuahua al Pacifico.

These three Benecke photographs, all taken in the mid-1870's, illustrate the beautiful lines of the diamond stacked 4-4-0 locomotives used by some of the early railroads. Top to bottom are the Kansas (Union) Pacific roundhouse in Armstrong, Kan. (now a part of Kansas City); three engines ready for the heavy snows of western Kansas (note the stacks of wood—engine fuel!) and freight engine No. 22.

The 50-mile-long Manhattan, Alma and Burlingame was built in the 1870's. Of the 1,300 railroads chartered in Kansas it was one of the few which actually laid track. In the mid-1880's it was sold to the Santa Fe which operated parts of the line until 1972. By 1976 the entire line had been abandoned. ▼

Benecke also photographed one of the little engines in front of the station and railway hotel at Wallace. Apparently tired of the long exposure required by wet plate photography one of the gentlemen at the left was recorded twice—as a man and as a ghost.

A subsidiary of the Santa Fe, the Chicago, Kansas and Western was built in the late 1880's. Originally the road was planned to have 2,400 miles of track, most of which was to be laid over Kansas in a giant cross. In reality it never was more than a Santa Fe feeder line. The train shown here was taking water from its fancy tank at Crosby, Wichita county, about 1890.

The Golden State Limited of the Chicago, Rock Island and Pacific was one of the crack trains of its time. Here it highballs through western Kansas about 1910.

Railway stations are terminals of adventure whether they be served by 25 trains a day or merely one. Shown on this page are typical Kansas depots at Nortonville on the Santa Fe, Oskaloosa on the Missouri Pacific, and Russell Springs on the Colorado, Kansas and Oklahoma.

Agents of the Missouri Pacific railroad depot at Horace, Greeley county, in 1914, take a brief time-out for the photographer.

Before the days of automation, freight of all kinds was unloaded by hand, as these grain handlers at Haysville demonstrate.

An unidentified locomotive photographed in central Kansas by F. A. Wesely.

Railroad stock was as richly engraved as it was expensive.

Railroad passes came in as many designs as there were carriers, and they have long been sought after by collectors.

Both railroad and fashion buffs should have an interest in this Benecke photograph of the "Kansas Pacific Railway Roundhouse at Ellis." While the former count the engines, the latter can study the stylishly-dressed matron seated in the foreground.

Early in January, 1912, western Kansas was covered with two feet of snow and ice. This train stalled near Minneapolis.

Rock Island section workers and their handcar at Kechi about 1900. The crew maintained the track and adjacent right-of-way for about 15 miles. Their work included straightening rails, laying new ties, tamping ballast and burning noxious weeds.

Train time at the Missouri, Kansas and Texas station in Emporia around 1915. Probably these travelers are taking a local to Junction City or Parsons to catch trains bound east or west, north or south. This particular branch line was abandoned in the 1950's.

Even the snow plow stuck fast in this southwest Kansas drift in the 1912 snow-storm. Manpower was then the only solution.

In the treeless areas of the West railroad trestles sometimes served as gallows. Here, suspended from the bridge over Fossil creek in Russell county, J. G. Burton, John Gay and William Gay "paid their debt to society" on January 14, 1894. It was even reported that one accommodating engineer up the line in 1868-1869 would move the morning train slowly over the trestle nearest the western Kansas town of Sheridan, wild and woolly but long since dead, in order that his passengers might see who had been hanged the night before. Below, loungers pose beside the Santa Fe paymaster's shed in Topeka.

69

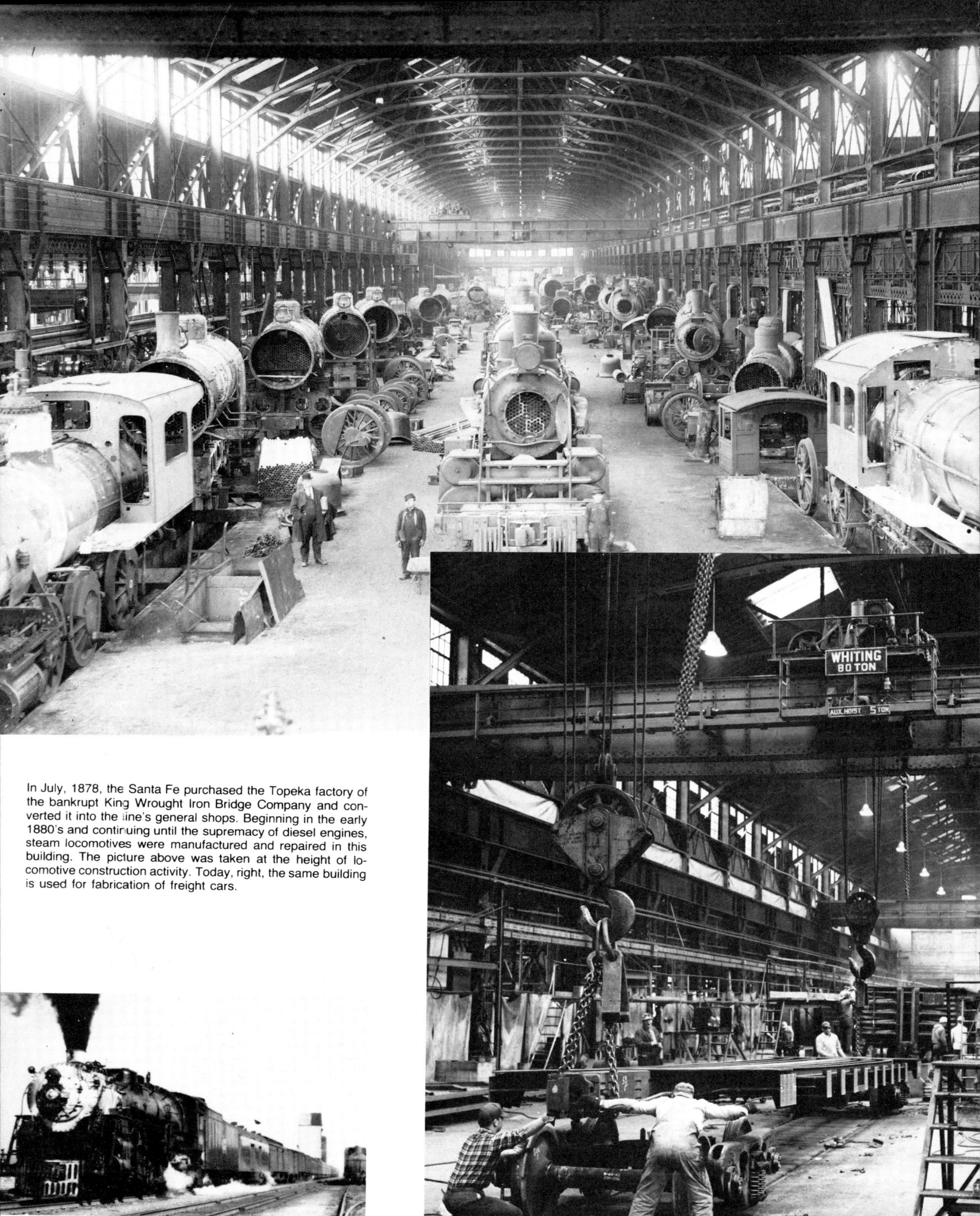

In July, 1878, the Santa Fe purchased the Topeka factory of the bankrupt King Wrought Iron Bridge Company and converted it into the line's general shops. Beginning in the early 1880's and continuing until the supremacy of diesel engines, steam locomotives were manufactured and repaired in this building. The picture above was taken at the height of locomotive construction activity. Today, right, the same building is used for fabrication of freight cars.

A Rock Island troop train bound from Fort Riley whistles through McFarland during the Korean War, 1952.

THE PASSING OF A NOSTALGIC ERA.— Steam locomotives and railroad operated passenger service disappeared from America's major lines within 20 years of each other. Recalling the romantic days of steam is the photograph, above, of a Rock Island passenger train as it pulls into North Topeka, where the line shared the depot facilities of the Union Pacific, probably in the late 1930's. Right, one of the Santa Fe's fine diesel-powered, lightweight passenger trains departing from Topeka on a frosty morning in the 1950's. Many Topekans felt the Santa Fe was the town's own and were especially pleased when passenger service began on April 26, 1869, with a two-car train filled with excursionists on an outing to Pauline, a distance of six miles. For over 100 years passenger service continued on the Santa Fe system, until April 30, 1971, when the famed CHIEF fleet, and other trains, were nearly all phased out and the remaining operations turned over to the quasi-governmental agency known as Amtrak. Two dozen or more Santa Fe passenger trains once made scheduled stops in Topeka each day, but this number dwindled to one Amtrak each way to Chicago and Houston.

Above, the dining room of Fred Harvey's Bisonte Hotel in Hutchinson in 1926. Fifty years earlier, in 1876, Harvey began in Kansas his long association with the Santa Fe railroad as purveyor of its food and oftentimes lodging services. Every facet of this service, which he spread up and down the line, was oriented toward Cleanliness, Comfort and Courtesy, bringing to him and his "Harvey House Girls" international acclaim. But Powell's restaurant, at left, on a Santa Fe subsidiary, the Chicago, Kansas and Western, early served meals in a converted baggage car. Eventually all major railroads offered on-train eating. Excellent food tastefully served, sparkling white tablecloths and napkins, polished silver, and monogrammed crystal contributed to the enjoyment of a meal consumed as the specially equipped dining car sped contented passengers over the rolling prairies. Below, lunching on a Union Pacific train about 1950.

A converted automobile supplies the motive power for the strange little "Sunflower Special" which probably operated on the tracks of the Kansas City, Wyandotte and Northwestern for short haul freight runs. This picture was taken while the train was on a siding at Valley Falls.

What appears to be a bus altered to fit a railroad was actually the Leavenworth and Topeka railroad's gasoline-powered No. 1, on a run (after 1918?) between those two towns. The L&TRR was a new name for the old Leavenworth and Topeka railway which was originally chartered in 1868, and operated for a time as part of the Santa Fe system.

Cars numbered 5 and 12 of the Arkansas Valley Interurban Railway Company were photographed, perhaps at Burrton, during the 1930's. The AVI was chartered in 1910 to connect Wichita, Newton and Hutchinson and to provide short-haul passenger, mail and small freight service. By 1942 the line was out of business.

Behold, the Gasoline Buggies

HOLD YOUR HORSES!—The invention of the automobile completely changed the life style of the American people. No longer was the individual solely dependent on public transportation for long trips or on horses for shorter journeys. Before the automobile was completely accepted and placed within the economic reach of all, horsedrawn vehicles had to share roads and streets with the new horseless carriages. In Dorrance on July 29, 1909, (above) the old warily faced the oncoming noisy, smelly new.

Pride of ownership is reflected in the faces of the Boeger and Warner families of Clay county as they pose in their new cars.

In the early days the driver had to be a mechanic as well. The group shown here was on a Bourbon county road.

Shining new Chevrolets of late 1920 vintage await buyers in Bill Brown's agency at Colby. They were priced at about $600 without such options as trunks and bumpers.

Many Kansas communities, after automobiles began churning up local roads, held "good road days," when the men turned out with teams and wagons to smooth and gravel lengths of highway. The ladies provided delicious food, while local business and professional men assisted in other ways. The group shown here repaired the streets of Linn about 1917.

Tractors were a great improvement over draft animals in road building. They had greater power to pull scrapers or graders, which could dig ditches, elevate the roadbed and smooth the whole thing down. Such an operation ordinarily did not require the services of four men on the grader, but men will be boys and the machines were fun to ride. This gang was at work in Greeley county in 1917.

Bricks, manufactured in Kansas, were used on countless city streets and even on cross country highways before macadamizing and concreting became practical. Bricks were laid by hand on prepared roadbeds and then firmed by the addition of sand or cement. The Reno county crew here seems to be adding a thin covering of concrete to a 1919 brick roadbed.

Kansans began oiling roads about 1906 and in 1907 the first macadamized highway was constructed north of Chanute. Late in 1914 the first concrete road in the state was under construction between Iola and Bassett in Allen county. From that time more and more state roads were hard topped until by 1976 all major thoroughfares were paved in two, four or six lanes. The concrete paving shown here, part of US highway 50, was being laid at Plymouth, Lyon county.

Motorcycles provided economical, if breath-taking, transportation for anyone who was willing to put up with their temperamental engines. Several makes were available. Shown here is a new Indian on display in Clay Center, perhaps about 1910.

As early as 1866 street car companies were incorporated to serve Atchison. In the following decades more than half a dozen were chartered though most never laid track. The situation was typical of many of the larger Kansas cities. For 40 years, beginning in 1895, the Atchison Railway Light & Power Company provided service to much of the town. Today it is part of the Kansas Power and Light Company. Here the motorneer, as he was called, and conductor of car No. 11 pause to have their picture taken with two small passengers.

Four of the six cars of the Union Street Railway Company which carried passengers in Winfield between Southwestern College and St. John's Lutheran, the railroad depots, the fairgrounds and other areas over ten miles of track. Incorporated in 1886, the line was mule-powered until 1909 when electric cars took over. These cars evidently were photographed near the end of the mule era.

To the Skies...

For centuries human flight has captivated the imagination of man. After the Wright brothers successfully demonstrated, on December 17, 1903, that heavier-than-air craft could fly, inventive Americans began to design their own planes. Two such people were William Purvis and Charles Wilson, of Goodland, who designed and patented a forerunner of the helicopter. The ship was built about 1910, but the engine was too small and it never flew.

Experimental aircraft were constructed in at least six Kansas towns by a dozen or more inventors. The Hunt Rotary airplane, shown here, was built at Jetmore in 1910. ▶

Henry L. Call, of Girard, constructed this airplane in 1908. Described as "a turkey with its wings clipped who wants to fly the coop and can't," the plane was destroyed by wind in March, 1909. Call built a total of 15 planes but only one flew and that crashed on its first flight. ▼

77

A. K. and E. J. Longren and William Janicke designed and built their first airplane in Topeka in 1911. On September 5 it made a perfect flight over the capital city and was named "Topeka I." By 1913 A. K. had become so proficient an aviator that he was making exhibition flights around the state, as advertised by the poster at right.

Several major aircraft producers got their start in Kansas. Below, Clyde Cessna, founder of Cessna Aircraft Company which in 1976 was producing more aircraft than any other manufacturer in the world, stands beside his 1917 Comet.

Air shows were popular after the first World War. One (below, center) took place near Wichita in the 1920's. At bottom, Karl Garver of Harper county was an early Kansas aviator whose Flying Circus planes are shown at La Crosse in October, 1920. The aircraft are two Laird Swallows, made in Wichita, and a Curtiss JN-4, the famous "Jenny" of the first World War.

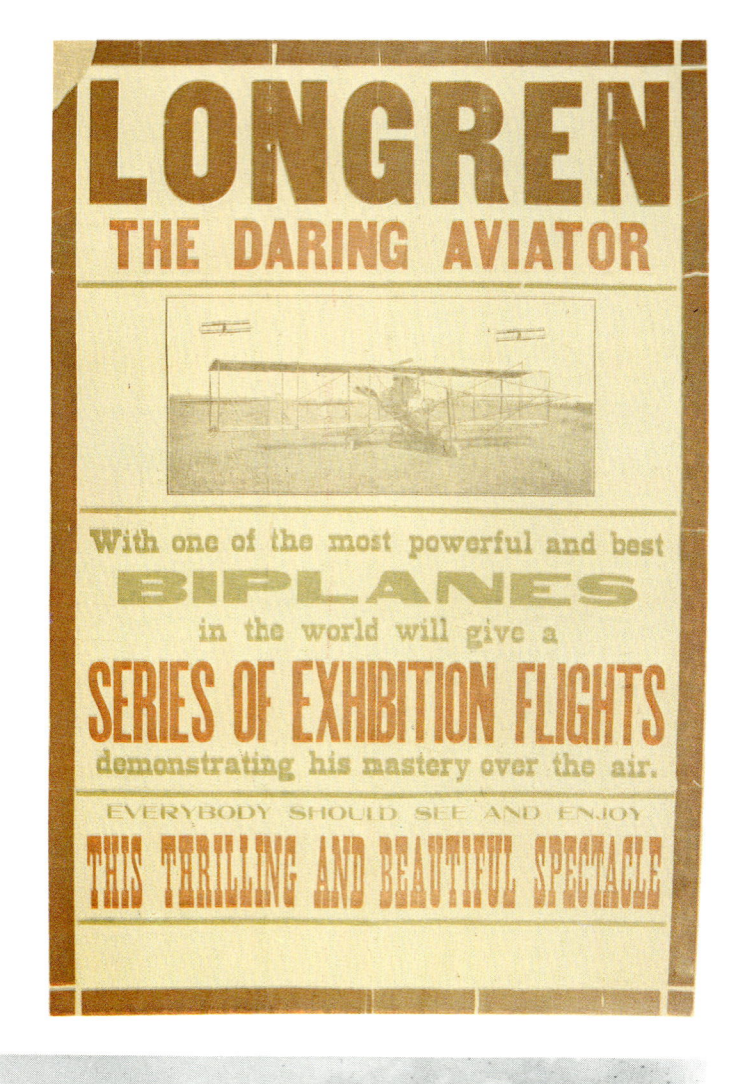

Pictured above are Lloyd Stearman (left) and J. Earl Schaefer (center) who were prominent in several early aircraft ventures. In 1927 they were listed as president and sales manager of Stearman aircraft in Wichita. Later Stearman became president of Lockheed and Schaefer general manager of Boeing's Wichita division. The division's fine World War II production record was largely due to his executive skill. Walter H. and Olive Ann Beech (left) view World War II production of AT-11 trainers at their Plant No. 1 in Wichita. Mrs. Beech headed Beech Aircraft Corporation after the death of her husband, leading it to a top position among small plane manufacturers. Fairfax airport at Kansas City, Kan. (below), was a typical busy Kansas terminal in the 1940's.

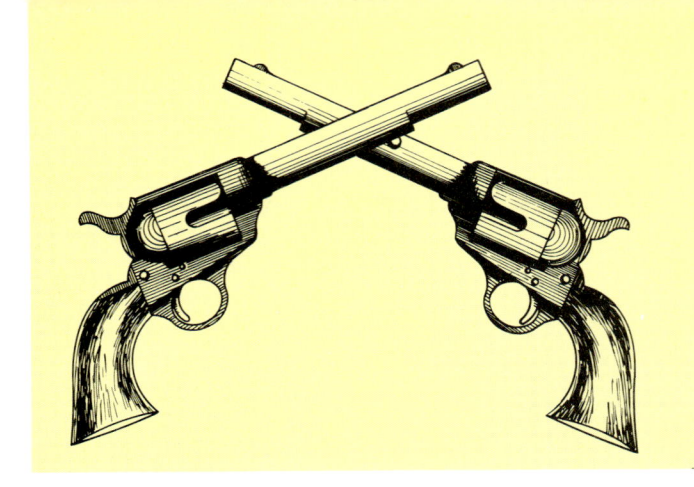

The Cowtown Frontier

Buffalo were fairly easy prey for hunters armed with the proper guns. By the time railroads crossed Kansas the animals were being killed by the thousands for their meat and hides. In the late 1870's they virtually disappeared from the state, but were partially replaced by Texas longhorns which were driven in great numbers up the Chisholm and other trails following the Civil War. Longhorns were used to stock Northern ranges and were also shipped from Kansas railheads to Eastern markets. One authority estimated that in the 20 years of the trail cattle industry about five and a half million head came up the various trails.

Where the trails met the railroads towns sprang up or quickly expanded. Hundreds of trail hands just off the long and weary trek up from Texas, their jeans jingling with three months' pay, were eager for rest and relaxation. Gamblers, dance-hall girls and saloon owners set up shop to relieve the cowboy of his hard-earned cash, and the drovers cooperated admirably. In the late 1860's to the mid-1880's in Baxter Springs, Abilene, Newton, Ellsworth, Wichita, Caldwell and Dodge City, and numerous other places such as Salina, Solomon, Bosland (Wilson), Brookville, Great Bend, Hutchinson, Junction City, and Russell, peace and order were often difficult to keep.

Some of the towns hired tough gunfighters such as "Wild Bill" Hickok, Wyatt Earp, "Bat" Masterson and others to hold the cowboys and the attendant businesses in check. Killings, wild cowboys and gambling halls were vividly described in the Eastern press. It was a time of romanticized adventure which still lives in the hearts of many. Advancing civilization and improved range cattle stock ended the big trail drives in the mid-1880's. The gunfighter sheathed his weapon and moved on to other frontiers. The cowtowns simmered down to become placid cities, or agricultural villages, or even ghost towns, and the wild and woolly cattle trail West was gone from Kansas.

Dotted in great numbers across the limitless expanse of the Great Plains were buffalo wallows, places where the "shaggies" rolled in the earth, covering themselves with dust or mud to ease the torment of flies, ticks and other insect pests. The one shown here was in Haskell county, but others are still to be seen over the state.

Before Dodge City earned its garters as Queen of the Cowtowns it was a booming depot for the shipment of buffalo hides, meat and bones. Charles Rath, a local merchant, here sits on a pile of hides estimated to contain 40,000 robes. The men in the background are operating a hide baling machine.

William F. "Buffalo Bill" Cody epitomized all that was romantic about the American West. Though he earned his nickname as a buffalo hunter he also served as a wagon driver, Pony Express rider, detective and Indian scout, all in Kansas.

Buffalo bones which had been left on the prairies by hunters more interested in hides and meat soon became an important product in the manufacture of fertilizer. Tons of the bleached bones were shipped to Eastern processing plants in the 1870's and 1880's.

Fresh buffalo skins were pegged to the ground for initial drying in this view of Dry Ridge, a Ford county water stop on the Santa Fe railroad. The dugout was typical of early dwellings in that treeless part of the state.

Texas Cattle Trails to Kansas Railheads

Delineating a general map of cattle trails would make most any cartographer throw up his hands in despair. As settlement filled the land, as railroads built west and south and as quarantine lines were reestablished cattle trails moved accordingly. In addition, scarcity of water and grass could cause a cattle trail to shift—up to several miles—at any time. This map attempts to show generally where the major cattle trails lay in Kansas. The Shawnee, Ellsworth and Ogallala trails particularly covered broad expanses of the Kansas topography from east to west as years went by. Thus, what is shown here may well be their routes during only a part of their existence.

From territorial days Kansas had laws against the importation of Texas cattle during the warm months of the year. The reason was that longhorns carried ticks which in turn bore splenic fever germs, highly infectious to domestic cattle. Quarantine lines shown on this map are those in effect during the height of the cattle shipping era. East and north of the lines Southern cattle could not be introduced into Kansas except during winter months. Some quarantine lines which did not effectively alter the restricted area are not shown nor is the 1885 line which closed the entire state. This prohibition, the growth of settlement and the range cattle industry effectively ended the trail cattle epoch of Kansas and American history. (It should be noted that the years shown on the map under major cowtowns represent their cattle trail periods.) This era (1866 through 1885) when an average of 270,000 head of longhorns was annually driven up from Texas to Kansas brought color to the fabric of our history:

Nowhere is that color better illustrated than in the diary of Abbie Bright, a young woman from Pennsylvania who settled near Clearwater, a few miles southwest of Wichita, in April, 1871. Abbie had come to Kansas to stake a claim on land three miles west of the Chisholm trail near that which her brother had settled on the year before. She was driven down the trail from Wichita, but had to cross the swollen Ninnescah river south of present Clearwater on top of boxes piled high on a freight wagon which had been delayed by high water. Her comments in the next few months (published in the *Kansas Historical Quarterly*, Topeka, in 1971) were vibrant with mentions of the continuous drama unfolding thereabouts. For example:

June 4, 1871: "The heavy rains raised the river, and a heard of cattle in crossing, stampeeded, and 15 or 20 were drownded. Every week 7 to 10 thousands of Texas cattle are driven north over the trail. If the cattle stampede, and dont want to cross the river, the hearders yell and fire off their revolvers. Sometimes we hear them here, and it sounds—as I suppose a battle does. It is the cattle that keep the trail worn so smooth. Their droppings are called 'cow chips,' and when dry, are burned by those who have no wood."

June 11, 1871: "There is a large herd of Texas cattle grazing South of here. It is not safe for a woman to be out where they see her. They would go for her. They have such big horns, they look frightful."

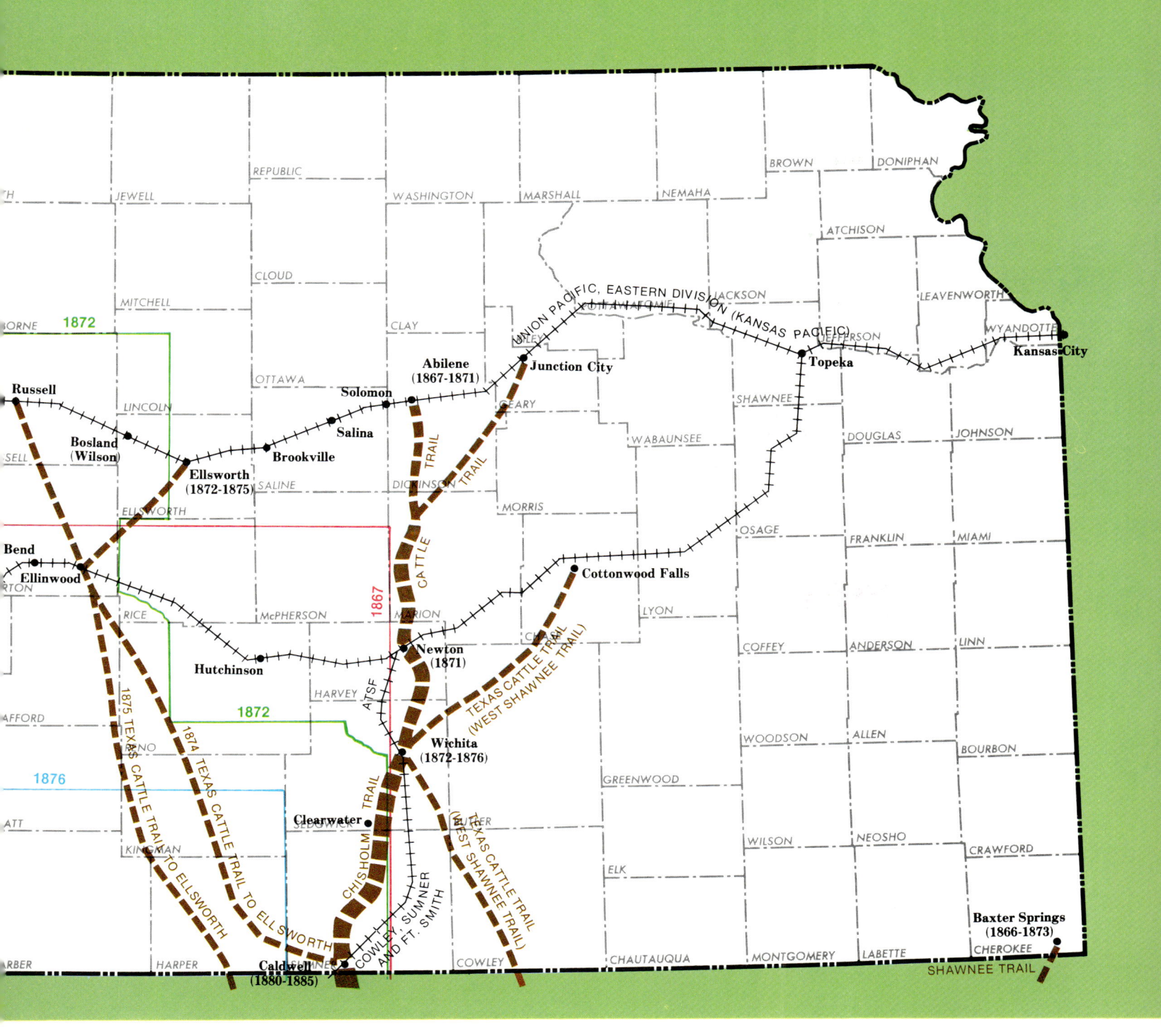

June 20, 1871: "While at R[oss's, a neighbor] four hearders came there horse back. One rode such a pretty pony. O, but I would like to have it. Rather wild looking men, with their revolvers in their belts. One of them was a Mexican. They have straight black hair, and dark complexins."

July 10, 1871: "They [the Taylor Markley family] are only half a mile from the [cattle] trail. [There, on] Sunday a. m. we saw coming over the divide a great heard of cattle I heard afterwards there was 2300 in the heard—and some hours later another heard and so it was all day. They crossed the river at the ranch and moved on toward Wichita. While we were eating dinner, we heard a noise, and some two dozen oxen [longhorns] had come over the river and were in her garden— We yelled— and with a broom tried to drive them away— Then they went to a corn patch, and it was not safe to leave the house—as they get cross— and their immense horns are wicked looking. Mr. Rose [Ross] told me he had seen steers whos hornes were five and six feet from tip to tip. He also said they were driven north— butchered, and the meat packed in their own hornes—and shiped to Chicago, Such yarns I hear a plenty. Well it was 4 p. m. when some men came riding a crost the river for the cattle, and in that time they had nearly destroyed two acres of corn."

July 19, 1871: "Yesterday morning I baked, then went a crost the River for plums. While picking them 6 hearders passed on horse back. There was no trail or path, they go just where they want to. I filled my pail, or bucket, started to waid back, when I saw all six, up the river in a sand bank, a couple were washing clothes, the others were pelting each other with sand. It is quick sand, and very moist."

September 3, 1871: "Thousands and thousands of Texas cattle, were driven north this Summer. Some have been allowed to graze on this side of the river before crossing."

On a cold day in mid-November, 1871, Abbie and her brother started to Wichita in a large wagon, via the Chisholm trail, and wrote: "After we reached the trail it clouded over, and became very windy. The trail was good traveling, yet the 20 miles to Wichita, in a big waggon was a long ride. The wind was so strong, it blew the dried cow chips on edge, and they rolled along on the trail like wheels. . . ." The Brights went on to the land office at Augusta where each completed the paper work and paid for his and her 160 acres of land, at $1.25 per acre.

"Holdin' the Herd at Abilene Town," a watercolor painted in 1969 by the late Byron B. Wolfe.

The advertisement at right appeared in the *Guide Map of the Great Texas Cattle Trail* which was published by the Kansas (now Union) Pacific in 1874.

James Butler "Wild Bill" Hickok was marshal of Abilene during 1871, its last and biggest year as a cowtown. He was still a young and inexperienced Kansas settler when the portrait (at left) was made in 1858.

Not all the dangers a cowboy faced were at trail's end. Flood, stampede, Indians, disease or some other cause may have been responsible for the death of the drover being buried here.

Looking west on Main street, Ellsworth, as photographed by R. Benecke about 1875. Drovers' Cottage may be seen in the distance to the left of the depot. It was in this street that the drunken Billy Thompson fatally wounded Sheriff Chauncey Whitney as the latter tried to disarm him. Billy was urged out of town by his brother Ben, who then stationed himself in the street and for a full hour dared the law to take him. "Where were the police?" growled the Ellsworth editor. Busy loading their muskets! About this time, so legend says, Prairie Rose, one of the girls from the shady area known as Nautchville, announced that she would ride a horse down this same street in the manner of Lady Godiva. At the appointed hour the cowboys and the saloon crowd appeared in great numbers. But because the gal rode sidesaddle, insists the legend, the cheer rose up from only one side of the street.

The same Main street, photographed from approximately the same angle 100 years later. Apparently only two or three portions of the old buildings remain, those just to the left of the figure in the foreground. The main business houses of Ellsworth long ago regrouped up North Douglas street, off to the right. The man standing at the right in the 1875 picture is unidentified, but the one in the 1975 photograph is an Ellsworth resident well-known over the state of Kansas.

During the height of Wichita's cowtown days, it also was an important sheep trading center as this 1873 photograph shows.

Mike and John Meagher, like the Mastersons and Earps, were brother cowtown peace officers in Kansas. Mike served as marshal of Wichita and mayor and marshal of Caldwell. John was sheriff of Sedgwick county and assistant marshal of Wichita.

"Mysterious Dave" Mather poses in his Dodge City assistant marshal's uniform (below). A few days after he left the police force, in July, 1884, Mather shot and killed his successor but was acquitted.

Dodge City's famed cowboy band, 1884.

The Dodge City Varieties, a dance hall located south of the deadline or Santa Fe tracks, about 1878. The bar tender is George Masterson, younger brother of the local sheriff, "Bat" Masterson.

Cowtown Characters

William L. "Billy" Brooks, marshal of Newton and badman of Dodge City, was hanged as a horsethief by Sumner county vigilantes in 1874.

"Rowdy Joe" Lowe, a cowtown character who lived up to his name in Ellsworth, Newton and Wichita.

"Timberline," a Dodge City dance hall girl.

"Squirrel Tooth" Alice, another of the Dodge City girls.

87

Ranching and Agriculture

The ranching boom that followed the trail drive era was at its height in the 1880's but a combination of bad weather and low prices later in the decade forced many ranchers out of business. However, Kansas continued to be a leader in cattle raising even though the open range gave way to more controlled pastures and feed lots. Field crop agriculture changed in the 1880's also. "Dry farming," which used cultivation to preserve moisture and prevent erosion, was studied by many Kansas farmers while others experimented with irrigation. Different crops were planted, supplementing corn and wheat—the staples—with the latter a hard, winter variety by that time. Soybeans, alfalfa, sugar beets and sorghum grains joined the list of marketable Kansas crops.

After working hard on the range all day, cowboys found the chuck wagon a refreshing and relaxing place to congregate. These men worked for the B. R. Grimes ranch, Clark county, around 1889.

A cowboy's dream, where women do the work and men sit back and watch! One author has written that "ideally, a branding party also includes a couple of pretty women. They add to the morale and are a great help in opening the beer. . . ." In this picture taken on the Lowe ranch near Scott City, the branding is being done by a woman while the vested gentleman at the right was looking after his thirst.

These hundreds of well-fed range cattle were on the Missing Brothers ranch near Ashland around the 1890's. After the decline of the trail-cattle industry and following the killing blizzard of 1886 most ranchers turned to blooded stock such as Angus and Hereford to build up their herds.

Mechanical and technological improvements in farm equipment permitted Kansas grangers to move quickly from dependence on hand tools (as this corn planter) to horse-drawn cultivators, to steam-powered tractors, and finally to "hurry-up" farming (as in the lower picture) when several tractors, run by internal-combustion engines, pulled gang plows. The latter photo was taken in Ellis county in the 1930's, but the locations and dates of the others are not known.

Kansans nurtured peach and apple orchards, beginning mostly in the 1870's, and grew melons in quantity where the soil was right. They raised sheep (even oldtime cattlemen found "woolies" could be tolerated and profitable), hogs, chickens and turkeys. By the 20th century farmers had diversified their products considerably and many would continue to do so even during the great wheat years of World War I when the up-to-then average acreage was greatly expanded "to win the war." Early in the 20th century Kansas agriculture was not the agribusiness of the 1970's, but neither was it just another 40 acres of wheat or corn on a small family farm.

The golden wheat fields of western and southern Kansas at harvest time seem to stretch from horizon to horizon, usually under a warm blue sky. Harvesting methods and machines changed greatly as more hundreds of thousands of acres came into production to make Kansas the bread-basket of the world.

An early binder which cut and tied wheat into bundles. These were quickly set up by harvest hands in shocks like those at the far right.

The threshing rig upon arrival would quickly get set with its drive belt in place. Men with pitchforks would already be out with hayracks, wide flat-bed wagons on which the bundles of wheat were loaded. Hauled to the separator, the bundles would then be pitched into the machine which would separate the grain from its chaff and straw. This Burket brothers' steam threshing rig, operating near Attica in the 1890's, was equipped with conveyor belts for straw disposal. Such belts were later replaced by more efficient blower pipes.

The separator measured the grain before dumping it into wagons through a movable spout. After hauling, the grain was then handshoveled into bins, or piled upon the ground to be reshoveled later (as in this Pratt county scene) when storage facilities were available.

Much of the hand work pictured above was eliminated with the coming of the combination harvester-thresher, three of which are shown here about 1930.

Watermelons, ripe and tempting, in a Washington county patch.

Processing sorghum on a Leavenworth county farm in the early years of the century.

The Northwood potato farm, Topeka, used its sacks to advertise its hometown.

Apples by the bushels, from a Doniphan county orchard, on their way to market.

Tall corn in Kansas (left). The elderly agriculturist (right) in Jefferson county, 1957, clings to the old ways as he gathers his corn.

Baling alfalfa, probably about the 1920's, and (below) an example of child labor in the sugar beet fields of western Kansas in the same period.

A good herd of mules, and a typical country school house are what one sees in this photograph which reached the State Historical Society some years ago. It came during an epidemic of country school reorganizations in Kansas which in effect closed the one-room school houses. Obviously it was this forced abandonment of neighborhood schools which is reflected in the descriptive caption someone inscribed on the picture (thoughtfully arrived at, no doubt): "A SCHOOL REORGANIZATION COMMITTEE."

Left, a striking photo from the "dirty thirties," a dust storm at Tribune, Greeley county, in 1933, and (below) a typical western Kansas farm in the early years of the century.

Mennonites, devout and pacifistic German-Russian Protestants, first came to central Kansas in the mid-1870's. One of their earliest settlements was Gnadenau, near present Hillsboro. They built houses like those they had in Europe, planted their hard winter wheat (Turkey Red), survived the elements and prospered. This drawing shows the Gnadenau people in temporary quarters at their planned village site.

C. B. Schmidt, the Santa Fe railroad's commissioner of immigration, who encouraged Mennonites to come to Kansas.

Bernhard Warkentin, miller of Red Turkey wheat in Halstead and Newton.

A Mennonite farm in Marion county several years later when agricultural success provided larger houses and more extensive farmsteads.

Large numbers of people with roots in Germany, other than the Mennonites, also came to Kansas. In the 1870's German-Russians who were Roman Catholic began to settle in Ellis, Russell and Rush counties, their communities marked by spired churches which could be seen for miles. One such family, living in Liebenthal, is pictured here.

German immigrants of the Lutheran persuasion also came. This is a wedding party at Cheney.

Leavenworth had a sizable German element in its population by the time of the Civil War. Most did not come directly from Germany to Kansas but moved on west from other already settled areas. This is a betrothal party at the home of Adolf Lange, Sr., in Leavenworth, about 1895-1896.

Ellis countians, some of them descendants of the original German-Russian settlers, at a picnic in 1920.

George Grant, Scottish silk merchant and founder of the British settlement at Victoria in 1873, introduced Angus cattle to Kansas. He is said to have made a large amount of money but died heavily in debt.

This is a combination hotel and depot built in 1873 on the line of the Kansas Pacific at Victoria. For a time it housed the British settlers who came to Ellis county as a result of Grant's promotion. Victoria was finally absorbed into the German-Russian settlement of Herzog but the English name continues to be retained.

One of the communities established by immigrants from the British Isles was Wakefield in Clay county. Begun in 1869, it had some unusual immigrants in a group of orphaned Londoners, who were sketched in New York in 1869, boarding the train for Kansas. The colonists suffered the usual pioneer hardships, and many gave up the struggle.

Another breed of Britishers, under the leadership of Francis J. S. Turnly, who had started a nearby ranch, took over a nine-year-old post office named Runnymede in northeastern Harper county and reestablished it in the town they founded in the vicinity in the winter of 1887-1888. Most of the time pleasure seemed to have priority over business, and no matter the season there were horse racing, steeplechasing, polo, and the pursuit of coyotes and rabbits in fox-hunting style. Football was also played, under English rugby and association rules, and Runnymede once challenged a Wichita team to a game which ended in a draw. Tennis was one of their sports, as illustrated by the above photograph labeled the Runnymede Tennis Club, but obviously it included all onlookers found thereabout. Thus the picture probably represents a good cross section of the some 100 colonists who were a part of the town during its brief five years of existence. The colony's Episcopal church pictured at right at Runnymede, was saved through its early removal to Harper where it presently houses museum relics relating to the church and the old town. Meanwhile what was once the townsite has long since become just another field of Kansas Wheat.

Among 20th century immigrants to Kansas were those of Mexican origin, most of whom came originally to work for the railroads. In recent years their bases of employment have broadened, but they have kept their traditions and customs alive. A picture taken in Garden City in 1975 represents that effort as these Americans-of-Mexican-descent and their neighbors gather for the annual September fiesta.

Best known of the black settlements in Kansas was Nicodemus, established in 1877 in Graham county. This photograph was probably taken in the early 1880's when business was beginning to flourish. As with many small towns in strictly rural areas the population of Nicodemus has dwindled and only a few blacks remain in residence today. However, three or four buildings from the town's more bustling years are still to be seen and the National Park Service in 1976 designated Nicodemus a National Historic Landmark.

Ho for Kansas!

Brethren, Friends, & Fellow Citizens:

I feel thankful to inform you that the

REAL ESTATE
AND
Homestead Association,

Will Leave Here the

15th of April, 1878,

In pursuit of Homes in the Southwestern Lands of America, at Transportation Rates, cheaper than ever was known before.

For full information inquire of

Benj. Singleton, better known as old Pap,

NO. 5 NORTH FRONT STREET.

Beware of Speculators and Adventurers, as it is a dangerous thing to fall in their hands.

Nashville, Tenn., March 18, 1878.

Handbills were circulated in the South by Singleton to recruit Negro settlers.

Benjamin Singleton, who encouraged blacks to leave the South for what he believed would be a better, more independent life in Kansas.

Edward P. McCabe of Graham county, Kansas state auditor, 1883-1887, is said to be the first black to be elected to high office in a Northern state.

Julia Lee, pioneer businesswoman, operated a store in Nicodemus.

One of the black settlements resulting from Singleton's efforts was Dunlap in Morris county. Negro families were still coming into the community in the 1890's but by the 1970's none of them remained. An academy, offering both the three R's and religious education, is pictured at right. The pupil in the foreground holds a sign, "God Bless Our School."

In 1893 the Rev. Charles M. Sheldon, pastor of Topeka's Central Congregational Church, opened a kindergarten for children from the black community. It was known as the "Tennessee Town Kindergarten" because many of the people had come to Kansas from Tennessee, and for many years was operated on a volunteer basis by interested Topekans. Pictured here (after 1900?) are some of the teachers and mothers of the kindergarten students. Today the city has absorbed much of what was old "Tennessee Town."

Doctor, Lawyer, Merchant...

From the moment Kansas territory was opened for settlement there were representatives of the business and professional worlds ready to buy and sell, counsel and cure. Some of the most prominent early Kansas leaders and town founders represented both worlds—Charles Robinson, for example, was a physician as well as a promoter of settlements. As new communities came into being storekeepers or skilled tradesmen were usually on the ground slightly ahead of the professions, although one could expect a lawyer, doctor and school teacher to arrive almost simultaneously. Here are pictures representing a variety of ways Kansans made a living in their towns, offering merchandise, skills and knowledge to each other and to the rural areas nearby.

D. R. Beckstrom practiced law from this office in Tribune.

Dodge City early boasted an active architectural office.

Will T. Beck poses proudly in the office of the Beck family's longtime newspaper, the Holton *Recorder*.

Dr. Homer B. Robison and associate practice dentistry in Ellinwood about 1910.

Dr. Robert E. Gray examines a patient in his Garden City office, 1901.

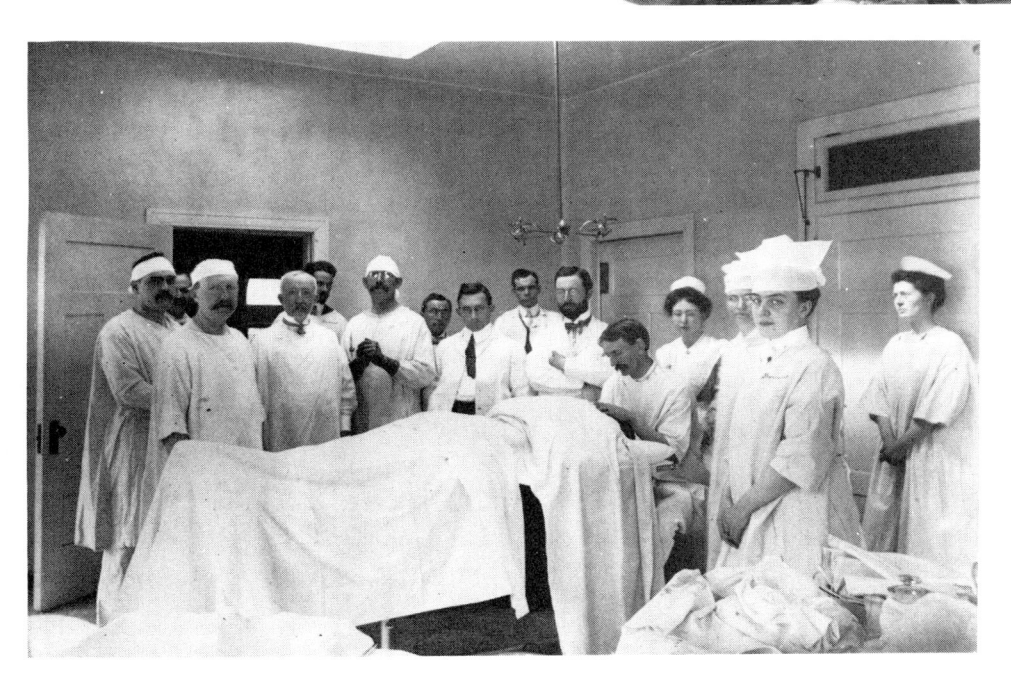

An operating room in the Jane C. Stormont hospital, Topeka, about 1900.

This unidentified Garnett bank rented "office" space to other businessmen.

During the Kansas territorial period the prevailing thought in America followed the Jacksonian view that the government should have nothing to do with banks and banking. Those banks which did exist were subject, therefore, to no federal regulations, and some made little pretense of guaranteeing the notes they issued. In Kansas, non-banking corporations were prohibited from engaging in any kind of banking activity and in 1857 private banks were specifically declared illegal unless they were chartered by the territorial legislature. Currency issued by banks and scrip issued by merchants, examples of which are shown here, often circulated at considerably less than par value. When Kansas became a state in 1861 the legality of banks was established by the constitution.

Shaves and a haircut in Valley Falls.

Cheney post office, 1915.

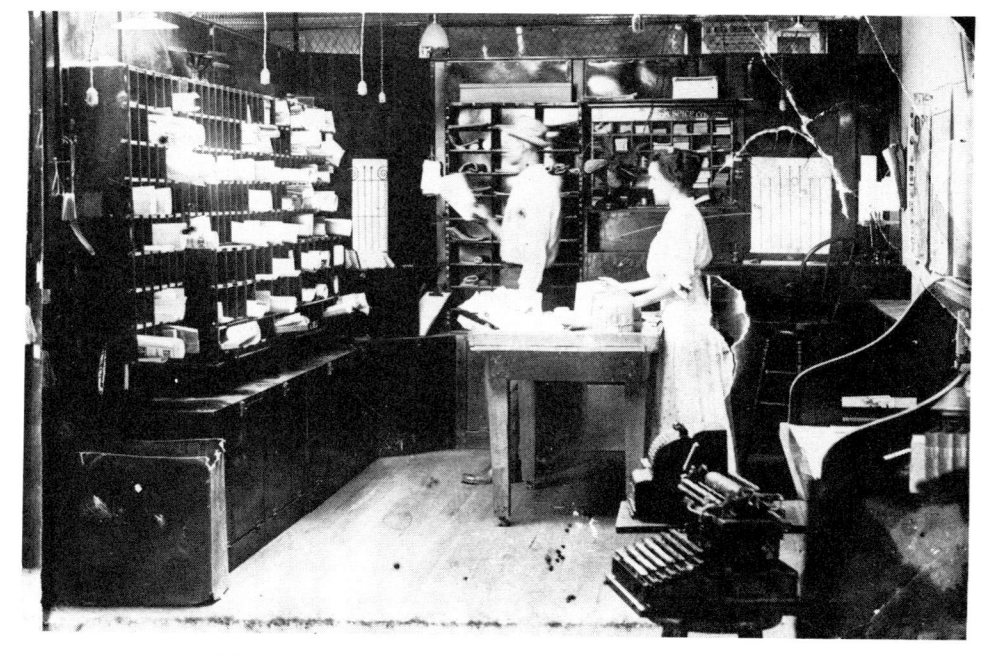

104

BANK STATE OF KANSAS
THREE DOLLARS
ATCHISON,
THE CITY BANK
ONE DOLLAR
ONE
KANSAS VALLEY BANK
Kansas State Savings Bank
NEMAHA COUNTY, KANSAS.
LAPPIN & SCRAFFORD
FIVE CENTS
SENECA.
Simpson Brothers Bank
ONE DOLLAR
Lawrence,
ONE
ATCHISON,
LAWRENCE
TWO DOLLARS
LAWRENCE BANK
ON DEMAND
KANSAS.
THE CITY BANK
Two Dollars
THE CITY BANK
THREE DOLLARS
STREETER & STRICKLER
THE BANK WM. H.R. LYKINS
THE LAWRENCE BANK
FIVE DOLLARS
LAWRENCE
KANSAS
STATE OF KANSAS
STREETER & STRICKLER,
TEN CENTS
JUNCTION CITY
ELDRIDGE BROTHERS,
LAWRENCE,
KANSAS.
TWENTY-FIVE CENTS,
ELDRIDGE BROTHERS,
THE LAWRENCE BANK
Three Dollars
LAWRENCE
KANSAS
THREE

B. E. Felible harness shop in Stockton, about 1923.

Traveling patent medicine salesman in Greenwood county.

C. E. Barr's Utica blacksmith shop around the turn of the century.

A Mulvane veterinarian believed in roadside advertising.

F. C. Zimmermann's hardware store in Dodge City.

Cutting ice from the Solomon river in Osborne county.

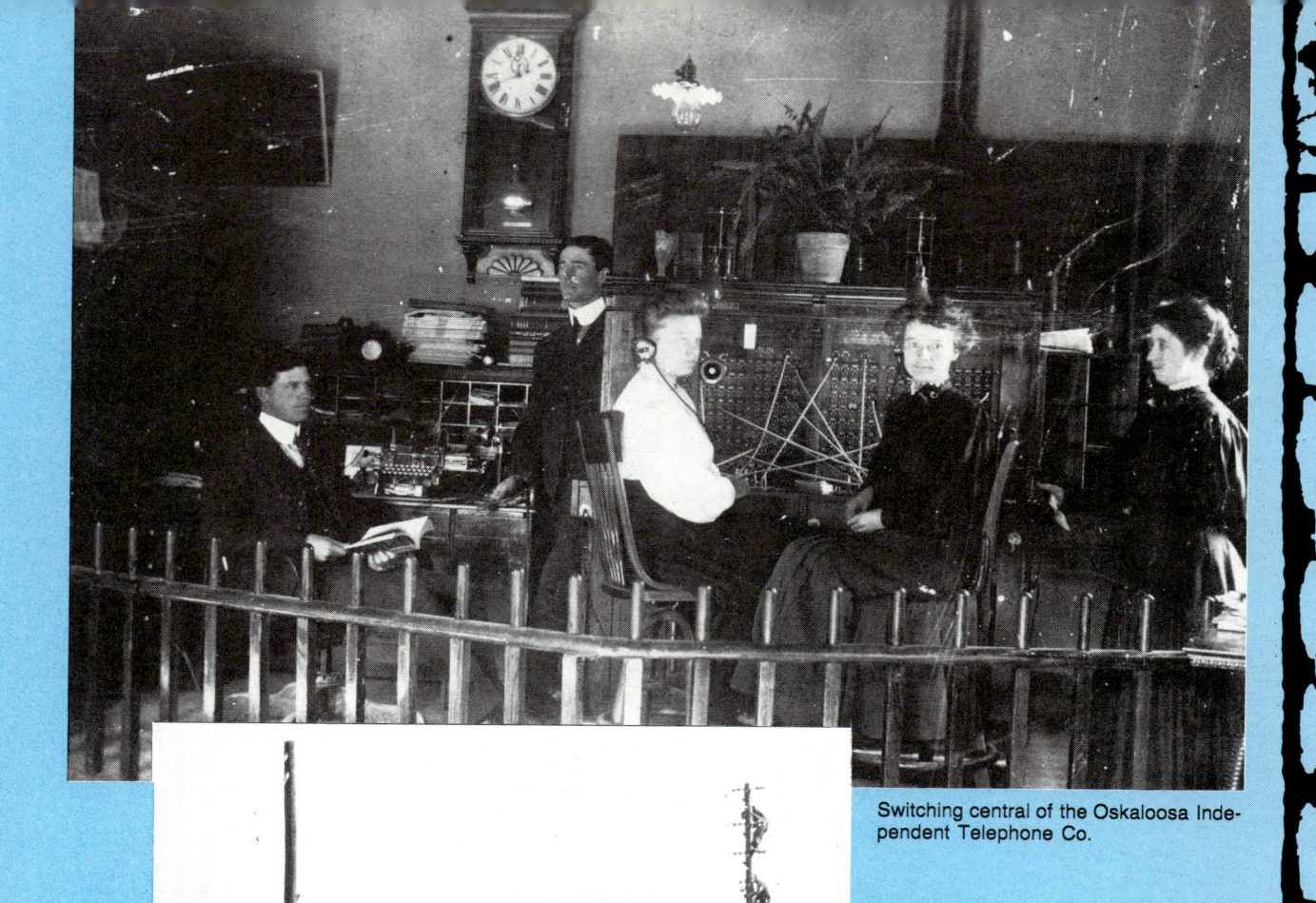

Switching central of the Oskaloosa Independent Telephone Co.

Brown county claimed what was said to be the first Kansas REA line, 1938.

A clothing store in Alma.

The Madden tailor shop in Dodge City.

Kingman tobacco store.

Stevenson's news stand in Wichita.

"Keep smiling" said the sign on the scales in this Garnett meat market.

A Lebo confectionery about 1910.

Max Weismiller's saloon in Marysville.

When five-cent hamburgers were available in Hutchinson.

The Loeb and Hallis drug store in Junction City.

J. O. McClay operated this Osawatomie grocery store in the 1920's.

The Williams and Kunkleman mill in Elk county.

A creamery in Colby.

Cutting lumber on the Larzerle farm, Doniphan county.

William Smith and his Abilene tin shop.

Broom shop in Hillsboro, 1926.

111

Culture on the Plains

Although life on the frontier often left little time for gracious living or the so-called finer things, there were always people in any community who early gave thought to education, religion and the arts. Some public education was provided for in the territorial years and churches were organized as quickly as congregations could be formed and a pastor obtained, on either a permanent or circuit-riding basis. Those same schools and churches often served as social centers, where people sang, danced, held debates and literary readings, presented plays and tableaux, and celebrated holidays.

Higher education was an early concern. Highland University began operation in May, 1857, and Baker University in November, 1858, with three state schools and several other private ones following in the next decade. In the larger towns dramatic groups and lyceums were organized, opera houses were built to accommodate traveling players and musicians, bands were formed, and singing groups ranging in size from quartets to Lindsborg's *Messiah* chorus were enthusiastically supported. These photographs are illustrative of some of those earlier cultural activities.

Settlers of the Caldwell-Bluff City area and their sod church, about 1880.

Parishioners gathered at a country church in western Kansas, probably about 1900.

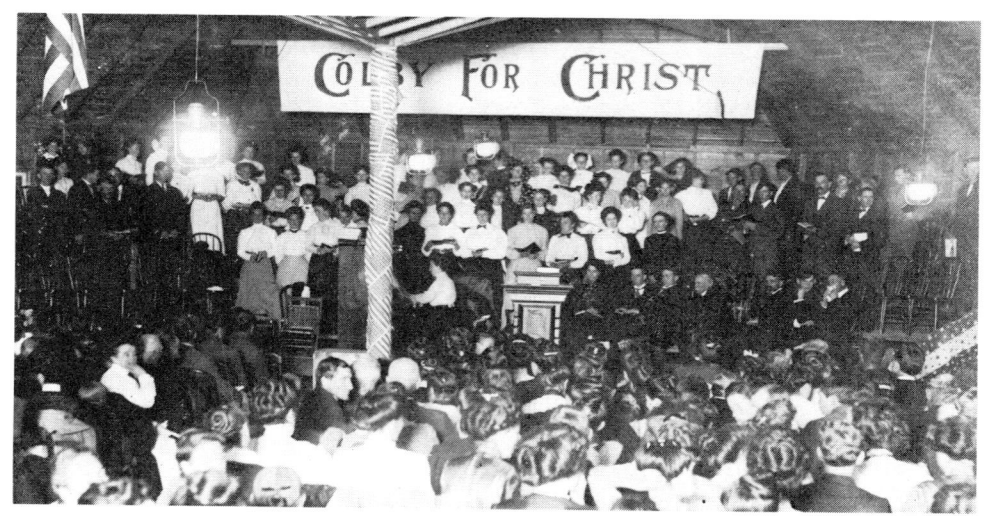

A full house for a Colby revival.

A stock tank serves as a baptistry near Linn, about 1915.

The Oskaloosa band. Concerts are still held in a bandstand in Old Jefferson Town at Oskaloosa.

Wakefield musicians on their bandwagon, 1899.

The Norcatur band, like those of other small communities, included musicians of all ages.

The Syracuse band, before a romantic stage backdrop, about 1900.

The Brown Grand Opera House, Concordia, as it looked when its main attractions were live performances. The building is listed on the National Register of Historic Places.

Dramatic group at the school house in Barclay, early 1900's.

"The Merchant of Venice" cast, on stage at Garnett.

The Messiah orchestra and chorus, Lindsborg, 1908.

The heating systems were similar in (1) Wichita and (2) Rice county school rooms in the late 1890's.

Algebra on a Tribune blackboard, 1908.

Kansas teachers studying during a "normal institute," early 1900's.

115

Thomas county students and their sod school, 1901.

The impressive new school at Eudora, 1879.

Mule and horse drawn buses drawn up before the Webster school.

A break from the routine at Montgomery county's Centennial school, 1892.

The Woman's Hesperian Club posed before their library at Cawker City. This building is now on the National Register of Historic Places.

116

Old Fraser Hall, of the University of Kansas, stands starkly on a barren Mount Oread in the 1870's.--Photo by R. Benecke.

Cooking class, Kansas State Agricultural College, 1890's.

Cooper (later Sterling) College students hard at their homework, 1913.

The impressively decorated Leavenworth Public Library, 1911.

117

They made their marks...

Many Kansas men and women have achieved distinction, and brought honor to their state, in various areas of productive endeavor. Also there have been some eccentrics whose activities have won notoriety, and these too are ours. A few—only a few—of the people who can be said to have "made their marks" are shown on this and several following pages. Others have been mentioned in earlier sections, and there are many more equally deserving who for reasons of space had to be omitted. But there will be other books of this kind in the Kansas future, and those who have been omitted from this may eventually expect to have their turn.

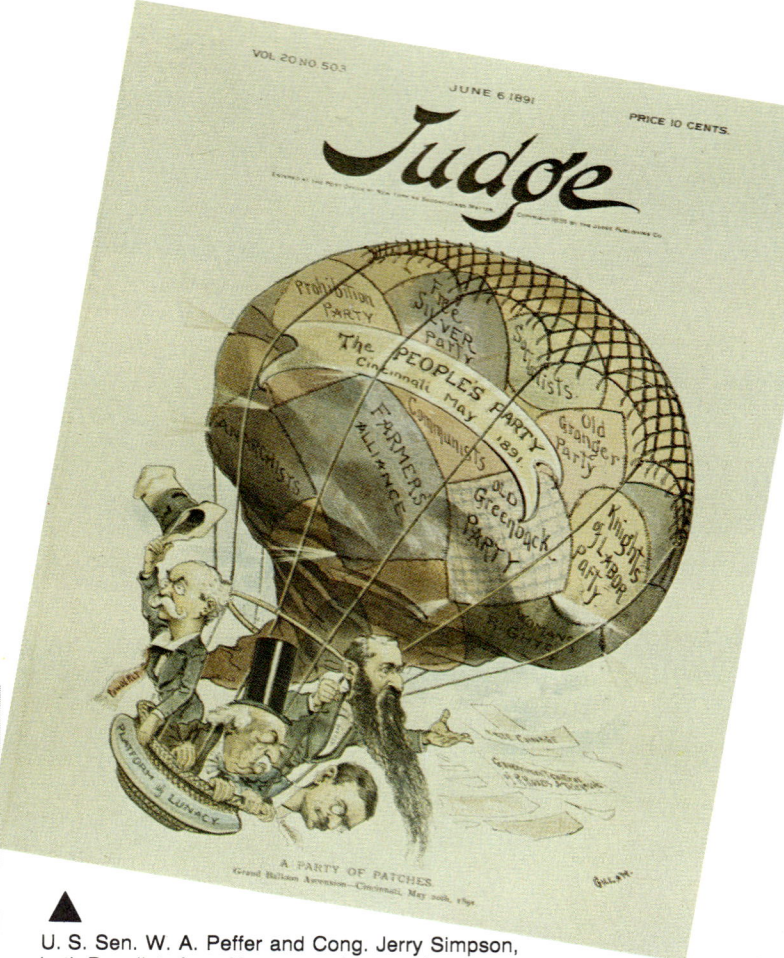

U. S. Sen. W. A. Peffer and Cong. Jerry Simpson, both Populists from Kansas, as featured in a cover cartoon by *Judge,* a popular humor magazine, June, 1891.

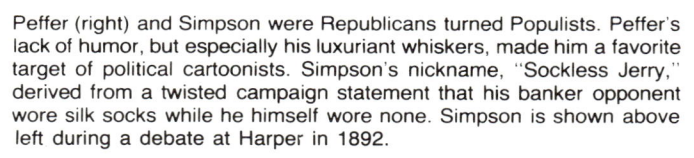

Peffer (right) and Simpson were Republicans turned Populists. Peffer's lack of humor, but especially his luxuriant whiskers, made him a favorite target of political cartoonists. Simpson's nickname, "Sockless Jerry," derived from a twisted campaign statement that his banker opponent wore silk socks while he himself wore none. Simpson is shown above left during a debate at Harper in 1892.

John J. Ingalls (left), a young man when this 1857 photo was taken, served as U. S. senator from Kansas from 1873 to 1891, when he lost his seat to Populist Peffer. Although Ingalls was one of Kansas' most erudite senators he failed to hold his following, and of him Eugene Ware wrote: "We think his epitaph should be: 'Up was he stuck, and in the very upness of his stucktitude he fell.'"

Right, a Populist parade in rural Dickinson county.

118

An Albert T. Reid sketch (left) shows Boston Corbett, famous as the slayer of John Wilkes Booth, Lincoln's assassin, providing a lively moment in the Kansas House of Representatives on February 15, 1887. Corbett had homesteaded in Cloud county in 1878, and was serving as an assistant doorkeeper. Declared insane and committed to the Topeka state hospital, he later escaped on horseback, never to be accounted for with certainty thereafter.

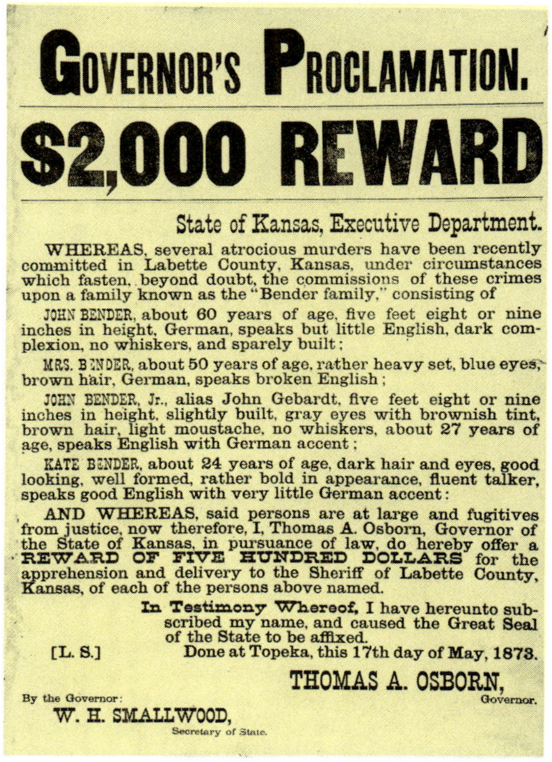

One of the most bizarre families ever to depart in haste from Kansas lived in northwest Labette county in the early 1870's. The family, the Benders, used their house as an inn and murdered and robbed several guests, burying the bodies in the garden. When a relative of one of those missing, following a cold trail, came upon the family he became suspicious and the Benders took flight. Here again their fate is not certain, but members of the posse who took after them were said to have remained unusually close mouthed forever after.

Off to jail again goes the militant Carry A. Nation (carry a nation for prohibition, she said), this time (above) in the custody of the marshal of Enterprise in 1901 after she and friends had entered a saloon to vent their wrath upon the characters and contents therein.

Maj. Gen. James G. Harbord, of Manhattan, was perhaps Kansas' most distinguished soldier in World War I.

At far left in car (about 1906) is "Fighting Fred" Funston who helped Cuba (1896-1898) gain her independence, became a hero while serving with the Americans in the Filipino Insurrection (1899-1901), and was commander of U. S. forces on the Mexican border in 1914-1916. The Funston family home near Iola, now a state museum, is on the National Register of Historic Places.

Emanuel Haldeman-Julius, who brought literature to the masses through his "Little Blue Books," at work in Girard in 1950, the year before his death.

Two nationally famous Kansas journalists, William Allen White (left), editor of the Emporia *Gazette,* and Edgar Watson Howe, editor of the Atchison *Globe.* In addition to their newspaper work, both were successful novelists and authors of many magazine articles.

Two Kansans, long prominent in politics: Arthur Capper (above left), publisher of the Topeka *Daily Capital* and several farm journals, who served as governor of Kansas and as U. S. senator, toiling at his desk on a hot July day in 1943 before air-conditioning made life more comfortable; and Charles Curtis (right), for many years congressman and senator, who was Vice-President of the United States under Herbert Hoover, the first person of Indian ancestry to hold the nation's second highest office.

Mrs. Susanna Madora Salter, said to be the first woman mayor of any U. S. community, was elected to that office by residents of Argonia in 1887. She and her husband, Lew, are shown here in their marriage photo, 1880.

Kansas suffragettes in Lawrence in the early years of the century.

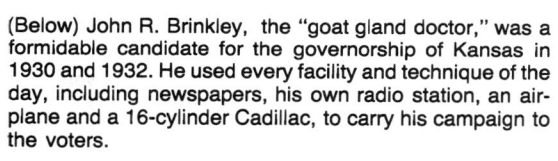

(Below) John R. Brinkley, the "goat gland doctor," was a formidable candidate for the governorship of Kansas in 1930 and 1932. He used every facility and technique of the day, including newspapers, his own radio station, an airplane and a 16-cylinder Cadillac, to carry his campaign to the voters.

Another Kansas campaigner was Alf M. Landon, who defeated Brinkley and incumbent Gov. Harry Woodring in 1932, and served two terms as governor. Landon was the Republican nominee for President of the United States in 1936, and is shown here addressing a crowd at Canton, Ohio, from the rear platform of his campaign train.

Former U. S. Sen. Harry Darby, of Kansas City, flanked by President Dwight D. Eisenhower and George Docking, first two-term Democratic governor of Kansas, obviously out on business relating to the development of the Eisenhower Center at Abilene, with which Darby was closely connected from its inception.

Though crippled by poliomyelitis, Thurlow Lieurance traveled much of the Western United States recording the music of 31 American Indian tribes. Reared in Neosho Falls, he lived in and out of Kansas until 1940 when he retired as dean of the fine arts department at Wichita University. He is most remembered for his composition "By the Waters of Minnetonka" which was published in 1912. Lieurance is shown here, probably in New Mexico, in the early part of the 20th century.

Georgia Neese Clark Gray, early engaged in the theater, succeeded her father as banker at Richland, was appointed treasurer of the United States under President Truman, and finally tapered off her banking career in Topeka sometime after her bank was removed from Richland when reservoir construction forced abandonment of the town.

Osa and Martin Johnson of Chanute and Independence (standing on plane), became internationally known explorers and photographers between the two World Wars. With still and motion picture cameras they recorded fast vanishing wild life in the South Pacific and Africa. Here, in Borneo in 1935, they chat with curious natives. Today the Johnsons are memorialized in Chanute's Safari Museum which interprets the heritage of the African tribes with which they were closely associated.

In 1932 Amelia Earhart Putnam, native of Atchison, became the first woman to fly the Atlantic alone. Other feats followed, including the distinction of being the first female to fly from California to Hawaii. In 1937 she attempted to circumnavigate the globe but was lost in the Pacific ocean. In the picture above she was participating in an Atchison parade in 1935.

Kansas novels made Topeka's Margaret Hill McCarter popular in the early 1900's.

Civil War nurse Mary Ann "Mother" Bickerdyke built a hotel in Salina in 1867.

Failing as a Kansas farmer, George W. Carver won fame as a teacher-scientist.

Noted populist orator Mary Elizabeth Lease, whose wit considerably enlivened the American political scene.

Adept at singeing political hides was Sol Miller, editor of the Kansas Chief, Doniphan county.

L. E. "Lizzie" Wooster, state superintendent of instruction (1919-1923), vowed to fire teachers who smoked.

Fred Harvey of Leavenworth made his Harvey Houses the ultimate in railroad dining.

David J. Brewer's distinguished legal career was capped by 21 years on the U. S. supreme court.

Charles M. Sheldon, Congregational minister, won international fame as author of the novel *In His Steps*.

Frederic Remington at Peabody in 1883 during an unsuccessful year as a Kansas sheep rancher. His fame as a great painter and sculptor of Western scenes came later.

Robert Merrell Gage, native Topekan, is a world renowned sculptor of Abraham Lincoln. His first Lincoln statue, upon which he was at work in a Topeka barn, was completed in 1918 and installed on the Kansas statehouse grounds where his statue of a pioneer mother was also placed in 1937.

Sven Birger Sandzen came to Lindsborg from his native Sweden in 1894 to teach at the recently founded Bethany College. All but eight years of the remainder of his long life were spent there. His bold paintings and block prints of Kansas and other landscapes won him international acclaim. He is shown above with two of his paintings in his Lindsborg studio in the 1940's.

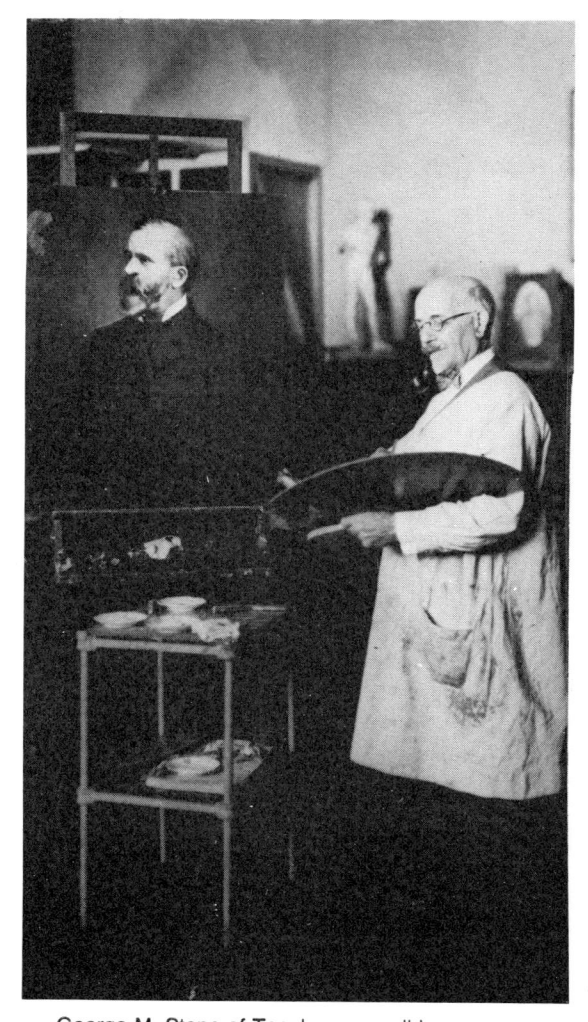

George M. Stone of Topeka was well known as a portrait and landscape painter around the turn of the century. In 1902 he and Albert T. Reid (right) founded the Reid-Stone school of art which later became the art department of Washburn University.

Albert T. Reid, born in Concordia in 1873, was Kansas' premier cartoonist from about 1896 to 1920 when he moved to New York. His pictorial comments on issues of the day ranged from the comic to the serious. Reid also did "real" painting, as he called it, and completed several murals as well as smaller canvases. George M. Stone painted this portrait of Reid as a wedding gift in 1902.

A noteworthy Kansas family—Mrs. Flo Menninger and the doctors Menninger. Mrs. Menninger, a Biblical scholar and teacher, is pictured here with her husband, Charles F. (second from right) and their sons William, Edwin and Karl. C. F. and Karl (far right) founded the Menninger Clinic in 1925, in which they were soon joined by William (left). Their clinic grew into the world famous Menninger Foundation. Edwin went into newspaper work but also became known for his books on flowering vines and trees.

Dr. Samuel J. Crumbine (at left), who practiced medicine in Dodge City around 1900, became secretary of the State Board of Health and leader of campaigns to stop the use of public drinking cups, roller towels and other germ-spreading practices. He finished his illustrious career in New York.

Dr. James Naismith (above), who invented the game of basketball at the International Y. M. C. A. Training School in Springfield, Mass., and in 1898 began a long career as director of physical education and coach at the University of Kansas, Lawrence.

Jess Willard of Emmett, Kan., knocked out Jack Johnson in the 26th round at Havana, Cuba, to win the heavyweight boxing championship of the world in 1915. The spectator in dark hat at far left is Bat Masterson, sports writer for the New York *Morning Telegraph* but better known as a frontier sheriff of Kansas' cowtown era. Four years later in Toledo, Ohio, Willard lost his title to Jack Dempsey.

125

Happiness is . . .

Before radio struck the public's fancy in the 1920's, and television's popularity beginning in the 1950's, recreational activities were more socially oriented than they are in 1976. Lyceums, taffy pulls, husking bees, sewing circles, holiday celebrations, quilting bees, spelling contests, and even funerals were reasons for persons to gather together for visits or gossip. Religious gatherings were also a common form of recreation on the frontier, for services often provided the only opportunity lonely

HAPPINESS IS . . . a family orchestra in Baldwin, going for a Sunday drive in Logan county, hearing the latest recordings in Ellis county or seeing the newest feature film in Ellsworth.

settlers had to visit with their distant neighbors. In the more settled areas, as might be expected, there were parties, dances, stage shows and other more formal recreations. There are as many sources of happiness as there are individuals. What is travail for one may be joy for another. To show, or even list, everything that has been used as recreation in Kansas would be impossible. The best that can be hoped for is a fair sampling of what Kansans did for entertainment, leisure and relaxation.

Watching a circus parade in Valley Falls, playing croquet at Sycamore Springs (Sabetha), celebrating the nation's birthday in South Haven or savoring a tasty barbecue in Linn county.

The great outdoors beckons Kansans to a tennis match in St. Marys, a 1905 skating party on Chapman creek, a boy scout campout near Cheney or a jaunt on an early version of a snowmobile at Oakley.

Cool Kansas water invites swimmers into North Cedar creek near Valley Falls, riders on an 1899 excursion boat on the Neosho, a quiet sail on a Sheridan county pond—1895, anglers at Burlington, and the Big One at Volland, early 1900's.

Games then intended for men only included billiards and bowling in Howard and a poker game behind the shingles in a Russell lumber yard. The ladies here in Osborne (1899) chat at a sewing circle meeting, and at Cottonwood Falls enjoy a Chautauqua gathering in a tent.

Street carnivals (in Valley Falls), dances (Leavenworth), a masquerade ball (Englewood), and May fetes (Fredonia) delighted the young and old of both sexes. Most of all, happiness is a well decorated Christmas tree laden with gifts for children of all ages.

Spectator sports—baseball at Humboldt in 1912 with Kansas' great Walter Johnson at bat, horse racing at Clay Center, basketball at Winchester high school in 1910, a football game probably between Washburn College and Ottawa, bronc riding at Scott City or automobile racing at Abilene.

Kansas Today

(82,264 square miles; population 2,314,479.)

Where everyone who resides in a city or town is still only a few minutes away from the open space of the country . . .

Where sunshine and blue skies on most days, blessed with sufficient rain much of the time, nurture bountiful harvests nearly every year . . .

Where more wheat is harvested than ever before, even with fewer farmers, and an enviable record as producer of one-fifth of the nation's crop is maintained . . . providing bread for the world . . .

Where the greens of growing grasses and crops are the prevailing country colors in the spring, followed by the harvest golds and browns of summer and autumn, and at year's end the dark green blades of winter wheat finally resting at ease until nudged by the warmth of spring to renew once more the growing cycle . . .

Where as many as six million head of cattle are on pasture simultaneously . . .

Whose industry and manufacturing now rival agriculture as the main source of income . . .

Where excellent schools and colleges, and churches, adequately and comfortably provide educational and religious needs for everyone . . .

Where water and other recreational areas and facilities are within easy reach of all . . .

THIS AND MORE IS KANSAS.

When the 45-man exploring expedition of Lewis and Clark headed up the Missouri river in the spring of 1804 one of the landings on their way West was at Kaw's mouth (presently Kansas City), on June 26. Thus they won the official distinction of being the first of the new Americans to set foot on land that became Kansas. The place was operating more under nature's rules in those years, for humankind had not yet arrived in numbers to festoon the area with clutter so noticeable today (see above). This hustle and bustle is not entirely representative of Kansas for, as the other pictures demonstrate, solitude and a communion with nature can still be experienced to any desired degree if the visitor will but follow into the setting sun the highways as they diminish from six lanes, to four, to two, to one.

Churches and Religious Services

Missionaries who brought religious teaching to the Indians were among the first whites to settle in the area that became Kansas. The religious zeal they inculcated long years ago continues today, for all major denominations are active in the state's urban and rural areas. However, records are not readily available as to the numbers each claims. The Roman Catholic church apparently is the largest with its 389 parishes and 320,991 members. The United Methodist denomination follows with 237,574 members.

(Above) St. Fidelis Catholic church, Victoria, called by William Jennings Bryan the "Cathedral of the Plains."

(Below) Interior, with wedding in progress.

(Right and below) Views of the United Methodist church in Olathe.

(Left and below) A royal visitor from Sweden, King Carl XVI Gustaf, appeared on the stage with Bethany's famed Messiah chorus while in Lindsborg on April 17, 1976.

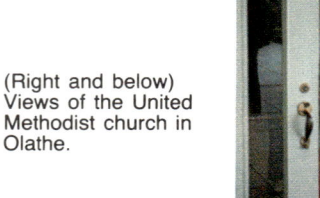

Colleges and Universities

Kansans have always been proud of their colleges, public and private. Some pioneer institutions of higher education eventually failed or were merged with stronger schools while others have gone through name changes but have remained continuously in operation. Today Kansas has three state universities, three state colleges and 17 private four-year schools. In more recent times the community junior college concept has been widely accepted and Kansas citizens now support 19 community colleges, four private two-year institutions, and a technical institute. Haskell American Indian Junior College, Lawrence, is federally funded, and Washburn University receives the bulk of its tax support from the city of Topeka.

Shown here are representative photographs from the current Kansas college scene. Washburn (top, left), which began as Lincoln College in Topeka in 1865, became a municipal university in 1941 but also serves many non-Topeka students. The main building of Friends University, Wichita (center, left), was far enough along in construction in 1888 to be occupied by its builder, shortlived Garfield University. From that time the structure has been one of Wichita's best known landmarks. After being vacant for a few years Friends University was established in the building in 1898. Friends currently receives church and private funding. Below is a 1975 aerial view of the state's largest educational center, the University of Kansas at Lawrence. Its buildings now blanket Mount Oread.

State Government and its Housing in Topeka

Since the beginning of statehood in 1861, Kansas government has grown in size, scope and budget and now provides services which were undreamed of at its inception. Although still living under the original constitution drawn up at Wyandotte in 1859, Kansans nevertheless have considerably altered the document through innumerable amendments. Kansas state government, now well into its second century, continues to operate conservatively with a minimum of scandal and fiscal irresponsibility.

State office housing changed from the original scrounging for any space available, including churches, in the 1860's, to a concentration of these departments and functions in the statehouse in the latter part of the 19th and half way into the 20th century. More recently many state offices and agencies are finding themselves again on the move to quarters around the city, as the statehouse becomes more and more reserved for offices directly relating to the governor and the legislature.

The Kansas capitol, popularly known as the statehouse, was built wing by wing from 1866 to 1903. It is a majestic building, as seen in the 1976 picture at left. Other photos show an interior view of the second floor, east wing, with a portion of the murals painted in the 1930's by native Kansan John Steuart Curry, and a view looking west across the south grounds, past the Lincoln statue by Robert Merrell Gage, another native Kansan, to the imposing state office building erected in 1956-1957.

The Kansas State Senate in session (east wing, third floor, of the statehouse).

A meeting of the Kansas House of Representatives (west wing, third floor, of the statehouse).

LOOK WHO CAME FOR LUNCH! Pres. Gerald Ford and nine Mid-West governors were luncheon guests of Gov. and Mrs. Bennett at the Executive Mansion on February 11, 1975. This picture shows President Ford, after arriving in a White House limousine, being greeted near the door by Governor Bennett. The men about them are not the other governors, but the President's security.

The Executive Mansion of Kansas is beautifully located near I-70 west of Topeka. Called Cedar Crest it has been the residence of Kansas governors since 1962. The property was a gift to the state from Mrs. Madge MacLennan, widow of Frank P. MacLennan, long-time publisher of the Topeka *State Journal*.

Gov. Robert Bennett holding a press conference in the Executive Suite in the statehouse.

An architect's drawing of the new Kansas Supreme Court building under construction south of the statehouse in Topeka. Scheduling called for the cornerstone dedication July 5, 1976, and the completion of the building in 1977.

Museums of History

And the Eisenhower Chapel,
"A Place of Meditation"

Several score Kansas history museums attract visitors from all over the world. Best known, perhaps, are those of the Eisenhower Center in Abilene, the State Historical Society in Topeka, and Fort Leavenworth. The National Park Service is restoring old Fort Scott and Fort Larned, and they are well worth seeing. Other smaller museums, many of high quality, are located throughout the state. For the main-street style of exhibits there are the re-creations of Front Street in Dodge City, Old Abilene Town, and Cowtown Wichita. A number of private museums and collections can be viewed by appointment. Indeed, there are museums in Kansas for almost every taste.

Since its completion in 1914 the state's Memorial building (above) has been headquarters for the Kansas State Historical Society and its famed Western collections. By the 1970's the building had become seriously crowded in all departments, and the Society has hoped for relief through the erection of a new building in which to rehouse its large museum and archeological divisions. This would permit expansion of the remaining departments, also with their constantly growing collections of Western and Kansas books, newspapers, archives, manuscripts, maps, and pictures, thus continuing the Memorial building as the state's "hall of records."

The Fort Leavenworth museum has many 19th century horse-drawn vehicles, two of which appear closeup in the picture above.

(Right) The Post Rock museum at La Crosse is built of a special limestone from which fence posts were fashioned by pioneers in the timber-scarce West. Among its exhibits the museum appropriately features the story of this rock and its many uses.

The Eisenhower Center at Abilene honors Pres. Dwight D. Eisenhower (above) and includes large areas of excellent museum exhibits, the Presidential library, and his boyhood home. Also there is the chapel (pictured at left), "A Place of Meditation," where President Eisenhower is interred.

Recreation

The technology which has shortened and lightened the work week of most Kansans has at the same time provided more recreation for their non-laboring hours. Air conditioned automobiles speed along well-maintained roads and streets carrying workers from offices to homes, to golf courses, tennis courts, or to weekend retreats. Federal reservoirs and state, county and city lakes make available boating, camping, skiing, fishing and swimming opportunities undreamed of in Kansas 25 years ago. Wildlife management techniques have brought back hunting as a major form of recreation. For those who prefer more sedentary activities there are theaters, concerts and restaurants, with television in most homes. Kansas of the 1970's easily provides for most of the recreational desires of its citizens.

Though primarily intended to conserve and control water, the state's 20 federal reservoirs with a shoreline of some 1,300 miles offer weekend campers, swimmers, fishermen, sailors and water skiers ample areas in which to indulge themselves. Attendant business adds hundreds of thousands of dollars to the Kansas economy.

Over the years the major Kansas basketball teams have generally led their conference peers. Annual contests between Kansas University and Kansas State University, the one above at Manhattan, involve thousands of loyal followers who consider these games the highlights of the winter season.

Sailboating on Lake Perry.

Fishing on the Chicaskia at Drury (above) or in most Kansas waters is improved through stocking by the Kansas Forestry, Fish and Game Commission as well as by individuals.

Pheasant, though not native to America, thrive in the fields of western Kansas to provide successful hunters' tables with succulent fare (above). Controlled shooting, forage and game management furnish hunters, such as the one pictured below in the Cheyenne Bottoms in Barton county, with exciting shooting. While deer and antelope have become available in recent years, most Kansas game still consists of small animals and fowl.

Manufacturing and Industry

In the 1950's Kansas ceased to be a predominantly agricultural state as its work forces turned more to industry. Manufacturing of all kinds blossomed with the Second World War and the trend has continued. Thousands of Kansans now work in factories which produce everything from dress patterns to multi-engined jet aircraft. Many towns of only modest population boast small industries which provide items essential to modern living. Larger cities like Topeka, Wichita and Kansas City are partly oriented to heavy industry, producing railroad cars, aircraft and automobile-related units. Mineral extraction continues to be an important facet of Kansas industry especially since the 1973 oil embargo placed new emphasis on domestic production of oil, natural gas and coal. Salt, gypsum, sand, Portland cement, limestone and clay, though limited in quantity, are principal assets in the Kansas economy.

The Hesston Corporation, a relatively new Kansas-born industry, has grown into an internationally prominent maker of automatic farm machinery, office furniture, waste disposal equipment and many other items. Its headquarters are in Hesston, Harvey county (see above).

An assembly section of the Coleman Company, a pioneer manufacturing concern of Wichita, which early became world known for its lamps, lanterns and stoves. In its continued expansion the company is also famous for other equipment relating to outdoor life.

In 1969 the McCall Pattern Company established a distribution center in Manhattan. Less than two years later the company, a division of the McCall Corporation which publishes one of the nation's leading women's magazines, transferred much of its pattern printing, cutting and folding operations to that city. A portion of the plant is shown above.

Because of the world's increased concern with energy sources, extraction and refinement of crude petroleum and the production of natural gas between 1974 and 1975 showed the largest worker percentage increase of all Kansas employment save the aircraft industry.

Kansas manufacturers account for over 70% of the world's private aircraft production and their planes are used around the globe. Portions of the Wichita production lines of four giants of the industry are shown here (left to right): Beech and Boeing, above, and Cessna and Gates Learjet, below.

Towns and Cities

Kansas towns have undergone drastic changes since the middle half of the 20th century. Employment opportunities have drawn more people to cities, causing some of the smaller towns to wither. In turn, downtown sections of larger cities encounter problems as outlying shopping centers proliferate. Revitalizing these downtown sections is a constant challenge. Many towns, however, continue their growth as progressive hubs of surrounding agricultural areas, or by securing new industries, or simply by serving as bedrooms and school centers for segments of nearby city populations who prefer small town living while retaining city employment.

Wichita (top), Fort Scott (center), and Holton (bottom) illustrate various approaches toward upgrading downtown business sections.

Farming and Harvesting

Modern equipment which allows one man to perform increasingly more work has caused the number of farms and farm workers in Kansas to decrease annually. Still, in 1975, Kansas could count 82,000 farms which were keeping 21½ million acres under cultivation. Irrigation, fertilizers, and weed and insect controls all contribute to increased yields per acre which make this state one of the major agricultural producers of the world. All this in spite of the fact that of the total Kansas civilian work force of slightly more than a million, less than 100,000 are engaged in agricultural pursuits.

Kansas farm pond near Emporia.

Cutting silage.

Irrigating corn in Doniphan county.

More than one-half the cultivated acreage in Kansas is put into wheat each year and the state consistently leads the nation in the production of this world-needed cereal. Visit Kansas in any June, and see these huge combines cutting wide swaths as they frequently work into the night, trying to keep up with the line of ripening wheat relentlessly moving north across the Plains states and on into Canada.

INDEX

Abilene 80, 84, 111, 122, 132, 139
Africa 122
Agricultural college. See Kansas State University, Manhattan.
Agriculture 88-93, 96
Aircraft 55, 77-79, 122, 142, 143
Aircraft industry 77-79, 142, 143
Alcove Spring, Marshall co. 17
Alfalfa 88, 92
Allen county 39, 75
Alma 108
Almena 44
Ambulances 56
American exploring expeditions 12
American Fur Company 17
Amtrak 71
Anderson, __ __ 48
Angus cattle 88, 98
Anthony 61
Apache Indians 27
Apples 91
Appleton 56
Arabs 5
Arapaho Indians 7, 27
Archaic period 2
Architects 102
Archuleta, Juan de 4
Argonia 121
Arickaree (Colo.), battle of the, 1868 28
Arickaree river, Colo. 28
Arkansas river 12, 13, 15, 27, 54
Arkansas Valley Interurban railroad 73
Armor (chain mail) 5
Armstrong 62
Artillery 35
Artists 124, 136
Ashland 56, 88
Asia 2
Atchison 8, 12, 13, 18, 61, 76, 122
Atchison and Cherry Creek Bridge and Ferry Company 18
Atchison *Globe* 120
Atchison Railway Light & Power Company 76
Atchison, Topeka and Santa Fe railroad 55, 60, 61, 63, 64, 69-73, 81, 87, 94, 96
AT-11 trainer (aircraft) 79
Athletes 125
Atlantic ocean 122
Attica 90
Aubry, Francis X. 14, 15
Augur, Gen. C. C. 27
Augusta 83
Automobile racing, Abilene 132
Automobiles 55, 74, 119, 126

Baker University, Baldwin 112
Baldwin 126
Band wagons 113
Bands 86, 113, 126
Bank notes 104, 105
Banks and banking 104
Baptisms, near Linn 112
Baptist mission, Johnson county 10, 11
Baptist mission, Shawnee county 11
Barbecues 127
Barber county 27
Barber shops 104
Barclay 114
Barr, C. E. 106
Barry, Louise 17
Barton county 141
Baseball 132
Basketball 125, 132, 140
Bassett 75
"Battle of the Arickaree, The" (Robert Lindneux painting) 28
Baxter Springs 80
Beck, Will T. 102
Becknell, William 14
Beckstrom, D. R. 102
Beech, Olive Ann (Mrs. Walter H.) 79
Beech, Walter H. 79
Beech Aircraft Corporation 79, 143
Beecher, Henry Ward 33
Beecher Bible and Rifle church 33
Beecher Island (Colo.), battle of. See battle of the Arickaree, 1868.
Beeler 41
Beginning of the West, The (book by Louise Barry) 17
Bell, Capt. John 13
Bender family 119

Benecke, R. 42-44, 62, 63, 67, 85, 117
Benkelman, Neb. 18
Bennett, Olivia (Mrs. Robert F.) 138
Bennett, Gov. Robert F. 138
Bering Sea 2
Bethany College, Lindsborg 124, 134
Bickerdyke, Mary Ann "Mother" 123
Bicycles 57
Bierstadt, Albert 20, 21
Big Blue (Mo.), battle of the, 1864 36
Big Blue river 13, 17
Big Creek 29
Billiards 130
Bison. See buffalo.
Black settlers 94, 100
Black troops 35
Blacksmith shops 106
Blue river. See Big Blue river, Little Blue river.
Blue river valley 94
Bluff City 112
Boating 129
Boeger family, Clay county 74
Boeing Company, Wichita 79, 143
Bohemian settlers 94, 95
Boissiere, Ernest Valeton de 94
Bolmar, Carl 19, 56
Bonner Springs 59
Boone, Daniel 13
Boone, Capt. Nathan 13
Booth, John Wilkes 119
Borneo 122
Bosland 80
Boston *Columbian Centinel & Massachusetts Federalist* 8
Bourbon county 74
Bourgmont, Etienne Veniard de 4, 6, 12
Bow and arrow 3
Bowling 130
Boxing 125
Boy Scouts 128
Brady, Matthew 60
Brewer, Justice David J. 123
Bright, Abbie 82, 83
Bright, Philip 82, 83
Brinkley, Dr. John R. 121
Broadsides, air show 78; Bender family 119; black immigration 100; cattle trail 84; stagecoach travel 57
Brooks, William L. "Billy" 87
Brookville 43, 80
Broom shop 111
Brown, Bill 74
Brown, John 32
Brown county 108
Brown Grand Opera House, Concordia 114
Bryan, William Jennings 134
Bryant, Edwin 17
Buffalo 1, 5, 16, 80, 81
Buffalo bones 81
Buffalo hides 81
Buffalo hunters 40
Buffalo hunting 5-7, 24, 29, 80, 81
Buffalo meat 18
Buffalo wallows 80
Bull, George 55
Bunker Hill 43
Burket brothers threshing rig, near Attica 90
Burlington 129
Burrton 73
Burton, J. G. 69
Butchering 52
Butler county 50
Butterfield, David A. 18
Butterfield Overland Despatch 18

Cabins 39
Caldwell 80, 86, 112
California 15, 17, 18, 122
California gold rush 15
Call, Henry L. 77
Camels 1
Camp Centre 22, 24
Camp Dunlap 25
Camp Mackay 22
"Camp of the Peace Commissioners at Medicine Lodge Creek" (Hermann Stieffel painting) 27
Camp on Pawnee fork 22
Camp Pond Creek 22
Camp Wynkoop 22
Campdoras, Dr. M. A. 20
Camping, weekend 140

Canada 8
Canadian river 5
Cantonment Martin 22
Capper, Arthur 120
Card games 130
Carl XVI Gustav, King of Sweden 134
Carnivals 131
Carpentry 53
Carson, Christopher "Kit" 14, 15
Cartoons 118, 119
Carver, George Washington 123
"Cathedral of the Plains." See St. Fidelis Catholic church, Victoria.
Catholic mission, Pottawatomie county 11
Catholic missions 10
Catholic settlers 94, 97, 98
Catlin, George 22
Cattle 17, 84, 88, 133, 146
Cattle trails, map of 82-83
Cawker City 116
Cedar Crest. See Executive mansion.
Celebrations 59, 95, 99, 127, 131
Cement 142
Centennial school, Montgomery county 116
Central Congregational church, Topeka 101
Central Overland California and Pike's Peak Express Company 18
Cessna, Clyde 78
Cessna Aircraft Company 78, 143
Cessna Comet (aircraft) 78
Chain mail 5
Chanute 75
Chapman creek 128
Chase county 146
Chautauquas 130
Cheney 52, 97, 104, 128
Cherokee county 45, 94
Cherokee neutral lands 9
Cherokee strip 9
Cheyenne Bottoms, Barton county 141
Cheyenne Indians 7, 24, 25, 27-29
Chicago, Ill. 71, 83
Chicago, Kansas and Nebraska railroad 61
Chicago, Kansas and Western railroad 63, 72
Chicago, Rock Island and Pacific railroad 55, 61, 63, 68, 70, 71
Chicaskia river 141
Chief (railroad train) 71
Chihuahua al Pacifico railroad 61
Chihuahua, Mex. 16
Chippewa reservation 9
Chisholm trail 80, 82, 83
Cholera 16, 25
Chouteau's Island 15
Christmas tree 131
Churches 99, 112, 134
Cimarron crossing, Santa Fe trail in Kearny county 15
Cimarron river 14
Circus 127
Circus parades 127
Civil War 23, 24, 26, 28, 35-37, 80, 97, 123
Clark, Georgia Neese. See Georgia Neese Clark Gray.
Clark, Capt. William 8, 12, 133
Clark county 56, 88
Clay 142
Clay Center 76, 132
Clay county 40, 74, 98
Clearwater 82
Clothing stores 108
Cloud county 119
Clymer, Rolla A. 146
Coal 142
Cody, William F. "Buffalo Bill" 81
Colby 74, 110, 112
Coleman Company, Wichita 142
Colorado 13, 19
Colorado, Kansas and Oklahoma railroad 64
Comanche Indians 5, 7, 27
Comet, Cessna (aircraft) 78
"Coming From Pike's Peak" (Samuel J. Reader painting) 20
Command and General Staff College, Fort Leavenworth 23, 139
Concord stagecoach 56
Concordia 114, 124
Conestoga wagons 58
Confectioneries 110
Conn, __ __ 40
Connecticut Kansas colony 33
Constitution hall, Lecompton 33

148

Cooke, Capt. Philip St. George 16
Cooper college. See Sterling College, Sterling.
Corbett, Boston 119
Corn 88, 89, 92, 145
Coronado, Francisco Vasquez de 4, 5, 12, 23
Cottonwood Falls 130
Cottonwood river valley 94
Council Grove 2, 16
Covered wagons 58
Cowboy band 86
Cowboys 85, 88
Cowles, 2Lt. Calvin 25
Cowtown Wichita 139
Cowtowns 80, 81, 84-87, 125
Creameries 110
Cretacian period 1
Crisfield 25
Croquet 127
Crosby 63
"Crossing the Kansas" (Alfred Jacob Miller painting) 17
Crumbine, Dr. Samuel J. 125
Cuartelejo band Apache Indians 5
Cuba 119, 125
Culture 112-117, 120
Curry, John Steuart 136
Curry murals 136
Curtis, Charles 120
Custer, Lt. Col. (Bvt. Maj. Gen.) George A. 24, 29
Custer, Libbie (Mrs. George A.) 29
Custer, Capt. Thomas 29
Czechoslovakian settlers 94, 95

Dance hall girls 87
Dance halls 87
Dancing 127, 131
Darby, Harry 122
Davis, Theodore R. 26
DeGolyer Foundation Library, Dallas, Tex. 43
Delaware reservation 9
Democratic party, Kansas 122
Dempsey, Jack 125
Dentists 103
Denver, Colo. 18, 19, 55
Depots 61-65, 68, 98
Dickinson county 118
Dighton 41
Dining cars 72
Dinosaurs 1
Docking, George 122
Doctors. See physicians.
Dodge City 14, 16, 26, 56, 57, 80, 81, 86, 102, 107, 109, 125, 139
Dodge City Bicycle Club 57
Dodge City Varieties 87
Dog Soldiers (Cheyenne Indians) 7
Dogs 5
Doniphan 6
Doniphan county 8, 11, 17, 20, 21, 91, 111, 123, 145
Donner party 17
Dorrance 74
Doy, Dr. John 33
Doy rescue party 33
Drovers' Cottage (Ellsworth hotel) 85
Drug stores 110
Drury 141
Dry farming 88
Dry Ridge 81
Dugouts 40, 51, 81
Dull Knife (Northern Cheyenne Indian) 24, 25
Dull Knife raid 23-25
Duncan, Patricia D. 146
Dunlap 101
DuTisné, Claude Charles 4

Earhart, Amelia. See Amelia Earhart Putnam.
Earp, Wyatt B. S. 80
Earp brothers 86
Earth lodges, Indian 3, 5
Education 112, 115-117, 135
1812 Overture (symphony by Peter I. Tchaikovsky) 48
Eisenhower, Gen. Dwight D. 122, 139
Eisenhower Center, Abilene 122, 139
El Cuartelejo, in Scott county 5, 12
Elk county 110
Ellinwood 103
Ellis 44, 67
Ellis county 89, 97, 98, 126
Ellsworth 43, 80, 85, 87, 126
Ellsworth county 12, 52, 95
Ellsworth trail 82
Emigrant Indian tribes 9, 23, 25

Emigration to the West 14-17, 20
Emmett 125
Empire City 45
Emporia 68, 145
Emporia *Gazette* 120
Englewood 131
English settlers 94, 98, 99
Enterprise 119
Entertainment 125, 127, 131, 132
Ethnic groups 94-101
Eudora 116
European settlers 94
Europeans 4, 23
Executive mansion, Topeka 138
Exodusters 94
Explorers 8, 12, 13, 122
Express and stagecoach lines, map of 18-19

Fairfax airport, Kansas City 79
Fairfield, Stephen H. 49
Fairway 109
Farm implements 89, 90, 92, 93
Farmers, prehistoric Indian 3
Farming 88-93, 96, 145
Fellible, B. E. 106
Ferries 55
Fifteenth Kansas volunteer cavalry 25
Fifth U. S. cavalry 27
Filipino Insurrection, 1899-1901 119
First American explorer of southern portion of the Louisiana Purchase 12
First capitol (Pawnee) 31
First concrete highway in Kansas 75
First drawing relating to Kansas 6
"First Furrow" (Seltzer painting) 38
First hotel in Dighton 41
First Independence day celebration in Kansas 8, 12
First Indian vice-president of the United States 120
First Kansas volunteer cavalry 35
First macadamized highway in Kansas 75
First Negro state auditor 100
First new American in Kansas region 8, 133
First passenger service on the Santa Fe railroad 71
First printer in Kansas 10, 11
First published reference to the sunflower 13
First rural electrification line in Kansas 108
First rural free delivery service in Kansas 57
First two-term Democratic governor of Kansas 122
First United Methodist church, Olathe 134
First U. S. infantry 24
First white man in Kansas 12
First white settlers in Kansas 134
First woman mayor in the United States 121
First woman to fly from California to Hawaii 122
First woman to fly the Atlantic alone 122
First woman treasurer of the United States 122
First World War. See World War I.
Fish 1
Fish, cretaceous 1
Fishing 129, 141
Flint hills 146
Football 99, 132
Ford, President Gerald 138
Ford county 51, 81
"Ford of the Little Blue, Kansas" (Albert Bierstadt photograph) 20
Forestry, Fish and Game Commission 141
Forsyth, Maj. (Bvt. Col.) George A. 28
Fort Atkinson 16, 22
Fort Aubrey 22
Fort Cavagnial 12
Fort Dodge 22, 26
Fort Ellsworth 22
Fort Fletcher 22
Fort Gibson, Okla. 22
Fort Harker 22, 27, 28
Fort Hays 22, 24-26, 28, 29
Fort Hays Kansas State College 1
Fort Kearny, Neb. 17
Fort Laramie, Wyo. 17
Fort Larned 22, 24, 139
Fort Larned National Historic Site 24
Fort Leavenworth 16, 17, 22, 23, 35, 36, 139
Fort Leavenworth-Fort Riley military road 18
Fort Leavenworth museum 139
Fort Mann 22
Fort Riley 15, 18, 22-24, 31, 70
Fort Scott (fort) 22, 23, 139
Fort Scott (town) 144
Fort Simple 37
Fort Union, N. M. 25
Fort Wallace 22, 28

Fort Zarah 22, 25
Fossil creek 69
Fourth of July. See Independence day.
Fox creek ranch, Chase county 146
Franklin county 32, 94
Fraser Hall, Kansas University 117
Fredonia 131
Freedman's Relief Association 94
Free-State constitution 33
Free-State hotel, Lawrence 31
Free-State movement 30-33, 38
Free-State victims 33
Fremont, Maj. Gen. John Charles 12, 13
French expeditions 8, 12
French settlers 94
French traders 4, 5, 12
Friends mission 10
Friends University, Wichita 135
Front Street replica, Dodge City 139
Frontier Historical Park, Hays 26
Funston, Maj. Gen. Frederick "Fighting Fred" 119
Funston family 119

Gaddis, John 24
Gage, Robert Merrell 124, 136
Garden City 99, 103
Gardner, Alexander 60
Garfield University, Wichita 135
Garnett 104, 110, 114
Garver, Karl, Flying Circus of 78
Gates Learjet Corporation 143
Gay, John 69
Gay, William 69
German Lutheran settlers 97
German-Russian Catholic settlers 97
German-Russian Protestant settlers 96
German-Russian settlers 94, 98
Gibbons, Robert O. 31
Gillicus arcuatus, a fish 1
Girard 77, 120
Glasco 18
Gnadenau 96
Godiva, Lady 85
Gogolin, Jacob 29
"Going to Pike's Peak" (Samuel J. Reader painting) 20
Gold rushes 15, 18, 20
Golden State Limited (railroad train) 63
Goodland 77
Gove county 1
Government, state 136-138
Graham county 94, 100
Grain handling 65
Grant, George 98
Gray, Georgia Neese Clark 122
Gray, Dr. Robert E. 103
Great American Desert 13
Great Bend 25, 80
Great Bend of the Arkansas river 12, 13
Great Plains 80
Great Smith (automobile) 139
Greeley, Horace 18
Greeley county 4, 64, 75, 93, 94
Greenwood county 58, 106
Grimes, R. B. 88
Grimes ranch, Clark county 88
Grocery stores 110
Guide Map of the Great Texas Cattle Trail 84
Gulf of California 61
Gunfighters 84, 86, 87
Gypsum 142

Haldeman-Julius, Emanuel 120
Halstead 96
Hamburger stands 110
Hancock, Maj. Gen. Winfield Scott 24
Hanover 15
Harbord, Maj. Gen. James G. 119
Hardware stores 107
Harness shops 106
Harney, Brig. Gen. (Bvt. Maj. Gen.) William S. 27
Harper 99, 118
Harper county 25, 61, 78, 99, 118
Hartford (steamboat) 54
Harvey, Fred 72, 123
Harvey county 142
Harvey Houses 72, 123
Haskell American Indian Junior College, Lawrence 135
Haskell county 80
Havana, Cuba 125
Haven 45
Hawaii 122
Hays 26, 60

149

Haysville 64
Health, Kansas State Board of 125
Helicopters 77
Hereford cattle 88
Herzog 98
Hesston 142
Hesston Corporation 142
Hickok, James Butler "Wild Bill" 80, 84
Hickory Point, battle of, Jefferson county, 1856 32
High Plains, The 5, 7
Highland 11
Highland University 112
Highway construction 55, 75
Highways 133
Hillsboro 96, 111
Hockaday, John M. 18
Hodgeman county 94
"Holdin' the Herd at Abilene Town" (Byron B. Wolfe painting) 84
Holladay, Ben 18, 19
Holton 102, 144
Holton *Recorder* 102
Holyrood 48
Homes 39-41, 48-52, 96
Homestead act 38
Hoover, Herbert 120
Horace 64
Horse racing 99, 132
Horses 1, 7, 17, 21, 74
Horton 61
Hospitals 103
Household activities 49, 52, 53
Houses 38-41, 48-51, 96
Howard 130
Howe, Edgar Watson 120
Humaña, Antonio Gutierrez de 4
Humboldt 39, 132
Hunnius, Ado 24
Hunt rotary airplane 77
Hunting 2, 3, 7, 29, 141
"Hurry-up" farming 89
Husking bees 126
Hutchinson, C. C. 60
Hutchinson 60, 73, 80, 110
Hyllningsfest (Lindsborg festival) 95

Ice age 1
Ice cutting 107
Ice skating 128
Immigration 94-101
In His Steps (book by Charles M. Sheldon) 123
Independence 122
Independence creek 8, 12
Independence Day 59, 127
Independence, Mo. 15-17
Indian campaigns 24, 27
Indian missions 10, 11
Indian motorcycle 76
Indian music 122
Indian removal 9, 10
Indian reservations 9, 10; map of 9
Indian settlements, early 2-9
Indian territory 5, 9
Indian treaties 25-27
Indian troubles 13, 16, 23-25, 27-29
Indian-white relationships 25
Indianola 56
Industry 142
Ingalls, John J. 118, 146
Interurbans 54, 55, 73, 76
Iola 75, 119
Iowa Indian reservation 9
Iowa, Sac and Fox Indians 9, 11
Iowa, Sac and Fox Presbyterian mission, Doniphan county 11, 20
Irish settlers 94
Irrigation 88
Irvin, Eliza (Mrs. Samuel) 11
Irvin, Rev. Samuel 11
Irving, Washington 13
Italian settlers 94

Janicke, William 78
Jefferson, Thomas 8
Jefferson county 32, 92
JN-4 "Jenny" (aircraft) 78
Johnson, Jack 125
Johnson, Martin 122
Johnson, Osa (Mrs. Martin) 122
Johnson, Rev. Thomas 10
Johnson, Walter 132

Johnson county 10, 58
Johnston, W. G. 15
Jones, John S. 18
Jones, Samuel 31
Jones, Russell & Company 18
Judge 118
Junction City 68, 80

Kansa dog dance 6
Kansa Indians 6, 7, 9
Kansas, admission of 34; maps of, back of front cover, 2, 6, 9, 12-15, 18-19, 30, 34, 82-83, back of rear cover
Kansas City 62, 79, 122, 133, 142
Kansas City, Mexico and Orient railroad 61
Kansas City, Mo. 36, 61
Kansas City, Wyandotte and Northwestern railroad 73
Kansas Historical Quarterly 82
Kansas house of representatives 119, 137
Kansas-Nebraska act 30, 34
Kansas Pacific railroad 15, 29, 42, 62, 67, 84, 94, 98
"Kansas Pacific Railway Roundhouse at Ellis" (R. Benecke photograph) 67
Kansas Power and Light Company 76
Kansas river 6, 8, 13, 54, 55, 133
Kansas senate 137
Kansas State Agricultural College. See Kansas State University.
Kansas State Board of Health 125
Kansas State Historical Society 11, 17, 20, 25, 26, 31, 93, 139
Kansas state militia 36
Kansas State University, Manhattan 117, 140
Kansas supreme court 138
Kansas territory, map of 30
Kansas University, Lawrence 140
Kaw Point 133
Kaw river. See Kansas river.
Kearny county 15
Kechi 68
Keyes, Sarah 17
Kickapoo Indians 9, 17
Kindergarten for blacks, in Topeka 101
King Wrought Iron Bridge Company 70
Kingman tobacco store, Kingman 109
Kinsley 16
Kiowa Apache Indians 7
Kiowa Indian tipis 7
Kiowa Indians 7, 26, 27
Konza Prairie preserve 146
Korean conflict 70

Labette county 119
La Crosse 78, 139
Laird Swallow (aircraft) 78
Lake Perry 140
Lake Scott State Park 5
Lamy, Rt. Rev. John B. 16
Lander, Col. Frederick West 20
Landon, Alf M. 121
Lands, public 38, 83
Lane, James H. 31
Lane county 41
Lange, Adolf, Sr. 97
Larzerle farm, Doniphan county 111
Last Indian raid in Kansas 23-25
Lawrence 17, 31, 33, 36, 38, 39, 42, 121, 125
Lease, Mary Elizabeth 123
Leavenworth, Brig. Gen. Henry 22
Leavenworth 18, 25, 72, 97, 123, 131
Leavenworth and Pike's Peak Express Company 18, 56
Leavenworth and Topeka railroad 73
Leavenworth county 12, 91
Leavenworth Public Library 117
Leavenworth *Times* 25
Lebo 110
Lecompton 32, 33
Lee, Julia 100
Lewis, Capt. Meriwether 8, 12, 133
Lewis, Col. William H. 25
Lewis and Clark expedition 8, 12, 133
Leyva y Bonilla, Francisco de 4
Liberal 12, 46
Libraries 116, 117
Liebenthal 97
Lieurance, Thurlow 122
Limestone, "Post Rock" 139
Lincoln, Abraham 119; statue of 124, 136
Lincoln College. See Washburn University.

Lindneux, Robert 28
Lindsborg 95, 112, 114, 124, 134
Link, John 39
Linn 75, 112
Linn county 37, 127
Little Big Horn (Mont.), battle of the, 1876 29
Little Blue Books 120
Little Blue river 20
Little Wolf (Northern Cheyenne Indian) 24
Livingstone, Dr. David 27
Lockheed aircraft company 79
Locomotives 62-65, 67-71, 73
Loeb and Hallis drug store, Junction City 110
Logan county 45, 48, 50, 55, 126
Long, Maj. Stephen H. 10, 12, 13
Longhorn cattle 80, 82-84
Longren, A. K. 78
Longren, E. J. 78
Louisiana 23
Louisiana Purchase 8, 12; map of 8
Lowe, Joseph "Rowdy Joe" 87
Lowe ranch, Scott county 88
Lumber cutting 111
Lutheran settlers 97
Lyceums 126
Lykins, Rev. Johnston 11
Lynchings 69, 87
Lyon county 75

McCabe, Edward P. 100
McCall Corporation 142
McCall Pattern Company 142
McCarter Margaret Hill 123
McCarty, Dr. T. L. 57
McClay, J. O. 110
McCoy, Rev. Isaac 10
McCoy, John 10
McFarland 70
McIntosh, Clint 55
MacLennan, Frank P. 138
MacLennan, Madge (Mrs. Frank P.) 138
McPherson county 5, 12
Madden tailor shop, Dodge City 109
Majors, Alexander 18
Mallet Paul 4
Mallet, Peter 4
Mammoths 1
Manhattan 6, 42, 52, 54, 119, 140, 142
Manhattan, Alma and Burlingame railroad 63
Manufacturing 142, 143
Maple Hill 57
Maps back of front cover, 2, 6, 8, 9, 12-13, 14-15, 18-19, 30, 34, 82-83, back of rear cover
Marais des Cygnes massacre 33
Marion county 96
Markley, Taylor 83
Marshall, S. W. 15
Marshall county 15, 17, 39, 50
Mary McDonald (steamboat) 54
Marysville 15, 17, 20, 110
Masquerade balls 131
Masterson, George 87
Masterson, William Barclay (Bartholomew) "Bat" 80, 87, 125
Masterson brothers 86
Mastodons 1
Mather, David "Mysterious Dave" 86
May fetes 131
Meagher, John 86
Meagher, Michael 86
Meat markets 110
Medicine Lodge creek 27
Medicine Lodge peace councils, 1867 26
Medicine Lodge treaties, 1867 27
Meeker, Rev. Jotham 10, 11, 17
Memorial building, Topeka 139
Menninger, Dr. C. F. 125
Menninger, Dr. Edwin 125
Menninger, Florence (Mrs. C. F.) 125
Menninger, Dr. Karl 125
Menninger, Dr. William 125
Menninger Clinic. See Menninger Foundation.
Menninger Foundation 125
Mennonite settlers 96, 97
Merchant of Venice, at Garnett 114
Messiah, at Lindsborg 112, 114, 134
Methodist mission, Johnson county 10
Methodist mission, Wyandotte county 10
Mexican border troubles, 1914-1916 119
Mexican settlers 99
Mexican war 14, 23

Mexico 12, 13, 15, 61
Miami Indian reservation 9
Militia, Kansas state 36
Miller, Alfred Jacob 17
Miller, Sol 123
Mills 91, 110
Mine creek, battle of, 1864 37
Minneapolis 3, 68
Minnesota 23
Missing Brothers ranch, Clark county 88
Mission Neosho 10
Missionaries 10, 11, 133
Missions, Indian 10
Mississippi river 9, 23
Missouri 6, 20
Missouri, Kansas and Texas railroad 68
Missouri Pacific railroad 55, 64
Missouri river 8, 12-15, 17, 18, 20, 54, 133
Montgomery county 116
Moravian mission 10
Morris county 94, 101
Motion pictures 126
Motorcycles 76
Mount Oread, Lawrence 117, 135
Mud wagons 56
Mules 93
Mullinville 46
Mulvane 107
Museums 139
Music 86, 113, 122, 126

Nation, Carry A. 119
National Historic Landmarks 10, 33, 100
National Park Service 23, 100
National Register of Historic Places 114, 116, 119
Natural gas 142
Nautchville 85
Nebraska 5, 9, 12, 15, 18
Neese, Georgia. See Georgia Neese Clark Gray.
Negro settlers 94, 100
Negro troops 35
Neosho county 10
Neosho Falls 122
Neosho river 129
Neosho river valley 2
Ness county 24, 41
New Mexico 16, 122
New Orleans 8
New York 98, 124, 125
New York Indian reservation 9
News stand 109
Newspaper publishers 102
Newspapers 25, 34, 102, 120, 123, 125, 138
Newton 73, 80, 87, 96
Nichols, Clarina I. H. 34
Nicodemus 100
Ninnescah river 82
Nomadic Indians 6
Norcatur 113
North Cedar creek 129
North Topeka 71
Northern Cheyenne Indians 24, 25
Northern Plains 25
Northwood potato farm, Shawnee county 91
Norton county 18, 40, 44
Nortonville 59, 64

Oakley 45, 128
Offices 65, 69, 102, 103, 108
Ogallala trail 82
Oil 142
Oklahoma 5, 9, 25, 26
Olathe 134
Old Abilene Town 139
Old Jefferson Town, Oskaloosa 113
Oñate, Juan de 4
Opera 114
Oregon 15
Oregon-California trail 14-17, 20, 21; map of 14-15
Osage Indian reservation 9
Osage Indians 6, 9
Osage Presbyterian mission, Neosho county 10
Osage river 6
Osawatomie 110
Osborne 130
Osborne county 107
Oskaloosa 64, 113
Oskaloosa Independent Telephone Company 108
Otoe and Missouri Indian reservation 9
Ottawa 17
Ottawa Baptist mission, Franklin county 17

Ottawa Indian reservation 9
Ottawa University 132
Overland stage line 18
Overland Stage to California, The (book by Frank A. Root and William E. Connelley) 19
Ox team freighting 16

Pacific ocean 8, 13, 122
Pack trains 54
Paget, Lord __ __ 29
Paleo-Indian dart points 2
Paleo-Indians 1, 2
Paola 46
Parallel road 18
Parsons 68
Patent medicine 106
Pauline 71
Pawnee, territorial capitol at 31
Pawnee fork 16
Pawnee Indian Village Museum 5
Pawnee Indian villages 5
Pawnee Indians 5, 7, 13
Pawnee pictograph 7
Peabody 124
Peace commissions 27
Pearson, Fred, family 58
Peffer, William A. 118
People's party 118, 123
Peoria and Kaskaskia Indian reservation 9
Philippine insurrection, 1899-1901 119
Phonographs 126
Physicians 102, 103, 125
Picnics 98
Pictograph, Pawnee 7
Pierce, Pres. Franklin 30
Pike, Capt. Zebulon Montgomery 12, 13
Pike's Peak 12
"Pike's Peak Emigrants, St. Joseph, Mo." (Albert Bierstadt photograph) 20
Pike's Peak gold rush 18, 20
Pike's Peak region 20
"Place of Meditation," Abilene 139
Plains, The 3, 13, 24
Plains Apache Indians 5
Plains Indian farmer period 2, 3
Plains Indian woodland period 2
Platte river, Neb. 13, 18, 27
Platte river stage route 18
Plesiosaur 1
Plymouth 75
Politics 118, 120, 121, 123
Polo 99
Pony Express 18, 19, 81
Pony Express station, Washington county 15
Pope, Gen. John 29
Popular sovereignty 30
Population, 1975 133
Populists. See People's party.
Post offices 104
Post Rock museum, La Crosse 139
Pottawatomie Baptist mission, Shawnee county 11
Pottawatomie Catholic mission, Pottawatomie county 11
Pottawatomie creek massacre 32
Pottawatomie Indian reservation 9
Pottawatomie Indians 9, 11
Potter, Theodore E. 17
Pottery, Indian 3
Powell's railroad restaurant 72
Prairie Dog creek 18
Prairie fires 19
Prairie Rose (Ellsworth dance hall girl) 85
Pratt county 90
Prehistory, Kansas 1, 2
Presbyterian mission, Doniphan county 11, 20
Presbyterian mission, Neosho county 10
Price, Maj. Gen. Sterling 36, 37
Prohibition 119
Proslave agitation 30-33, 38
Proslave Indians 5
Protestant settlers 94-99
Pueblo, Scott county 12
Purvis, William 77
Putnam, Amelia Earhart 122

Quantrill, William C. 36
Quantrill's raid on Lawrence 36
Quapaw strip 9
Queen of the Cowtowns. See Dodge City.
Quilting bees 126
Quivira 4, 12

Racing 132
Railroad construction 60
Railroad depots 61-65, 68, 98
Railroad dining cars 72
Railroad offices 65, 69
Railroad passes 67
Railroad restaurants 72
Railroad roundhouses 62, 67
Railroad section crews 61, 68
Railroad shops 70
Railroad stock 66
Railroads 54-56, 60-73, 84, 87, 98
Ranches 88
Range cattle industry 80, 82, 88
Rath, Charles 81
Reader, Samuel J. 20, 32, 36
Recreation 126-128, 130, 132, 140
Reeder, Andrew H. 31
Refineries 142
Reid, Albert T. 119, 124
Reid-Stone School of Art 124
Religion 3, 112, 126, 134
Remington, Frederic 124
Reno county 45, 75
Representatives, Kansas house of 119
Republic county 5
Republican band of Pawnee Indians 5
Republican party 118, 121
Republican river 18
Republican river stage route 18
Republican river valley 94
Reservations, Indian, map of 9
Restaurants 72
Reynolds, P. G. 56
Rhinoceros 1
Rice county 5, 115
Richardson, Albert D. 18
Richland 122
Riley, Bvt. Maj. Bennet 14, 15
Rio Grande, headwaters of 12
Robinson, Dr. Charles 31, 32, 102
Robinson, Sara T. D. (Mrs. Charles) 31
Robison, Dr. Homer B. 103
Rock Island railroad. See Chicago, Rock Island and Pacific railroad.
Rock mountains 12, 15, 17, 19
Rodeos 132
Roman Catholic church 134
Roman Nose (Cheyenne Indian) 24, 28
Root, Frank A. 19
Ross, William 83
Roundhouses, Kansas Pacific 62, 67
Rugby 99
Runnymede 99
Runnymede Tennis Club 99
Rural electrification 108
Rural free delivery service 57
Rush county 29, 97, 139
Russell, William H. 18
Russell 44, 80, 130
Russell county 51, 69, 97
Russell Springs 64

Sabetha 127
Sac and Fox Indians of Mississippi reservation 9
Sac and Fox Indians of Missouri reservation 9
Sacramento, Calif. 18, 19
Sailboating 140
St. Fidelis Catholic church, Victoria 134
St. George 42
St. John, John P. 94
St. John's Lutheran College, Winfield 76
St. Joseph, Mo. 15, 17-20, 33
St. Louis, Mo. 42
St. Marys 54, 128
Salina 80, 123
Saline county 12
Saloons 110
Salt 142
Salter, Lew 121
Salter, Susanna Madora (Mrs. Lew) 121
Sandzen, Sven Birger 124
Santa Fe, N. M. 14-16
Santa Fe railroad. See Atchison, Topeka and Santa Fe railroad.
Santa Fe trail 14-16, 20, 24-26; map of 14-15
Satanta (Kiowa Indian) 26, 27
"Satanta Addressing the Peace Commissioners" (Hermann Stieffel painting) 27
Say, Thomas 13
Scandinavian settlers 94

Schaefer, J. Earl 79
Schmidt, C. B. 96
Schools 93, 101, 115, 132, 133, 135
Scotch settlers 98
Scott, Maj. Gen. (Bvt. Lt. Gen.) Winfield 23
Scott City 5, 88, 132
Scott county 5, 12, 25
Sculptors 124, 136
Second World War. See World War II.
Section hands 61, 68
Sedgwick county 58, 86
Seltzer, O. C., painting by 38
Settlement, early white 38
Seventh Kansas cavalry 35
Seventh U. S. cavalry 24
Sewing circles 130
Seymour, Samuel 6
Sharps arms 33
Shawnee Baptist mission, Johnson county 10, 11
Shawnee county 20, 56
Shawnee Indian reservation 9
Shawnee Methodist mission, Wyandotte county 10
Shawnee Methodist mission and manual labor school, Johnson county 10, 31
Shawnee Sun 11
Shawnee trail 82, 83
Sheep 86, 89, 124
Sheldon, Rev. Charles M. 101, 123
Sheridan 28, 40, 69
Sheridan county 129
Sierra mountains 15
Silkville 94
Simpson, Jeremiah "Sockless Jerry" 118
Singleton, Benjamin "Pap" 94, 100, 101
Siouan speaking Indians 6
Sioux Indians 28
Siwinowe Kesibwi. See *Shawnee Sun.*
Sixth U. S. infantry 15
Skating 128
"Skimmer of the Plains." See Francis X. Aubry.
Sleighs 58
Smallpox 25
Smith, Jacob 41
Smith, William 111
Smoky Hill river 27
Smoky Hill river stage route 18
Smoky Hill valley 94
Snively, Col. Jacob 16
Snowmobiles 128
Sod churches 112
Sod houses 40, 41, 48
Sod schools 116
Solomon 80
Solomon river 107
Solomon river stage routes 18
Sorghum grains 88
Sorghum mill 91
"Sound on the Goose" 38
South Haven 127
South Pacific 122
Southwestern College, Winfield 76
Soybeans 88
Spanish expeditions 4, 5, 7, 8, 12
Spelling contests 126
Sphynx, The, Gove county 1
Sports 125, 132
"Squirrel Tooth" Alice (Dodge City dance hall girl) 87
Stage lines, map of 18-19
Stage shows 127
Stagecoach travel 18, 19, 54, 56
Stanley, Henry M. 7, 27
State Office building 136
Statehouse 136-138
Steamboats 54
Stearman, Lloyd 79
Stearman aircraft company 79
Steeplechasing 99
Sterling College, Sterling 117
Sternberg Memorial museum 1
Stevenson's news stand, Wichita 109
Stieffel, Hermann 27, 28
Stockton 106
Stone, George M. 124
Stores 106-110
Stormont hospital, Topeka 103
Storms 68, 69, 93
Street carnivals 131
Street railways 55, 76
Suffragettes 121
Sugar beets 88, 92
Sumner county 87

Sunflower Special (railroad train) 73
Sunflowers, first mention of, in Kansas 13
Surveyors 10, 60
Swallow, Laird (aircraft) 78
Sweden 124, 134
Swedish settlers 94
Swimming 129, 140
Sword, Coronado officer's 4
Sycamore Springs, Sabetha 127
Syracuse 113

Taffy pulls 126
Tailor shops 109
Taylor, N. G. 27
Tchaikovsky, Peter I. 48
Teachers 102
Telegraph lines 18
Telephone companies 108
"Tennessee Town" kindergarten, Topeka 101
Tennis 99, 128
Tenth U. S. cavalry 28
Terry, Gen. A. H. 27
Texas cattle 80-84
Texas cattle quarantine lines 82; map showing 82-83
Texas, Republic of, disputes its boundary with the U. S. 16
Theaters 114, 126
38th U. S. infantry 60
Thomas county 40, 116
Thompson, Benjamin "Ben" 85
Thompson, William "Billy" 85
Threshing 90
Tigers, saber-toothed 1
"Timberline" (Dodge City dance hall girl) 87
Tin shops 111
Tobacco stores 109
Toledo, Ohio 125
Topeka 11, 16, 42, 49, 51, 69-71, 78, 91, 101, 122, 124, 135, 136, 142
Topeka *Daily Capital* 120
Topeka *Kansas Tribune* 34
Topeka I (aircraft) 78
Topeka state hospital 119
Topeka *State Journal* 138
Topolobampo, Mex. 61
Town building 38, 61
Town shares 46, 47
Towns 42-46, 85, 100
Track laying, UPED railroad 60
Trails, 14; maps of 12-15, 18-19, 82-83
Trails, cattle 80, 82-85; map of 82-83
Transients 54
Transportation 54-79
Treaties 26
Tribune 93, 102, 115
Truman, Harry S. 122
Turkey Red (hard winter) wheat 96
Turkeys 89
Turnly, Francis J. S. 99

Ulibarri, Juan de 4
Union (Eastern division, and Kansas Pacific) railroad 15, 18, 19, 42, 55, 60, 62, 71, 72, 84
Union Street Railway Company 76
United Methodist church, Olathe 134
United States cavalry training center, Fort Riley 24
United States supreme court 123
United States troops 14-16, 23-25, 35, 37, 60
University of Kansas, Lawrence 117, 125, 135
Utica 106

Valley Falls 73, 104, 127, 129, 131
Veterinarians 107
Victoria 98, 134
Village Indians 3-6
Villasur, Pedro de 4
Viscarra, Col. Jose Antonio 15
Volland 129

Waddell, William B. 18
Wagons 46, 54, 57-59, 106, 126
Wagons, wind 55
Wakefield 59, 98, 113
Wallace 63
Walnut creek 25
Ware, Eugene 118
Warkentin, Bernhard 96
Warner family, Clay county 74
Washburn College. See Washburn University.
Washburn University 124, 132, 135
Washington county 15, 20, 91
Water recreation 140

Water skiing 140
Watermelons 91
Waterpark, Lord ___ ___ 29
"Waters of Minnetonka, By the" (song by Thurlow Lieurance) 122
Waugh, Henry W. 22
Wea and Piankeshaw Indian reservation 9
Webster 116
Weddings 97, 134
Weismiller, Max 110
Wellington 56
Wells, Fargo and Company 19
Welsh settlers 94
Wesely, F. A. 48, 65
Western Kansas gold strike. See Pike's Peak gold rush.
Western cattle trail 82
Westmoreland 15
Weston, Mo. 17
Wheat 88-90, 96, 99, 133, 145
Wheat harvesting 90, 145
White Plume (Kansa Indian) 6
White, Wlliam Allen 38, 120
White Cloud and Troy *Kansas Chief* 123
White-Indian relations 23-25
Whitney, Chauncey B. 28, 85
Wichita 5, 48, 73, 78-80, 82, 83, 86, 87, 99, 109, 115, 139, 142-144
Wichita county 63
Wichita Indians 4, 5
Wichita State University, Wichita 122
Wichita University. See Wichita State University, Wichita.
Wilkinson, Lt. James B. 12
Willard, Jess 125
Williams and Kunkleman mill, Elk county 110
Wilson, Charles 77
Wilson 43, 80, 95
Wilson's creek (Mo.), battle of, 1861 35
Winchester 132
Wind wagons 55
Winfield 76
Wolf creek or river 17
"Wolf River, Kansas" (Albert Bierstadt painting) 20, 21
"Wolf River Ford, Kansas" (Albert Bierstadt photograph) 20, 21
Wolfe, Byron B. 84
Woman's Hesperian Club, Cawker City 116
Woman's rights 121
Wood cutting 53, 111
Woodland Indians, Eastern 3
Woodring, Harry H. 121
Wooster, L. E. "Lizzie" 123
World War I 78, 89, 119
World War II 79, 142
Worrall, Henry 16, 37, 94
Wright brothers 77
Writers 120, 123, 125
Wyandotte 54, 136
Wyandotte constitution 34, 136
Wyandotte county 10
Wynkoop, Col. Edward W. 24

Xiphactinus molossus, prehistoric fish 1

Young Men's Christian Association Training School, Springfield, Mass. 125

Zimmermann, F. C. 107

Topeka, Kansas, June 6, 1976

Kansas—the 34th Star was produced by the staff of the Kansas State Historical Society under the official sponsorship of the State of Kansas:

Governors

Robert B. Docking, Arkansas City, 1967-1975.   Robert F. Bennett, Overland Park, 1975—.

Presidents of the Senate

Robert F. Bennett, Overland Park, 1972-1974.   Richard D. Rogers, Manhattan, 1974-1975.
Ross O. Doyen, Concordia, 1975—.

Speaker of the House

Duane S. McGill, Winfield, 1972-1976.

Also cooperating with the state was the Kansas American Revolution Bicentennial Commission:

Chairmen

Morris J. Krouse, Wichita, 1972-1975.   Warren W. Shaw, Topeka, 1975-1976.

Members

Gray Breidenthal, Kansas City, 1973-1975.
Dudley T. Cornish, Pittsburg, 1974-1976.
Mrs. Robert B. Docking, Arkansas City, 1973-1975.
John D. Montgomery, Junction City, 1973-1974.
John G. Montgomery, Junction City, 1974-1976.

Mrs. Harold E. Robbins, Kansas City, 1973-1976.
James H. Shaver, Goodland, 1973-1976.
Homer E. Socolofsky, Manhattan, 1975-1976.
Nestor R. Weigand, Jr., Wichita, 1973-1974.
Mrs. Beatrice Jacquart Williams, Dodge City, 1975-1976.

Secretary

Nyle H. Miller, Topeka, 1972-1976.

Executive Directors

John M. Taylor, II, Wichita, 1973-1975.   Charles D. Stough, Lawrence, 1975-1976.

Administrative Officers

Mrs. Ernestine Fatzer, Wichita, 1972-1975.   Mrs. Charlotte M. Olander, Topeka, 1975-1976.

Executive Secretaries

Mrs. Carol Dodds, Wichita, 1974-1975.   Mrs. Rozan Zweifel, Topeka, 1975-1976.

KANSAS
BICENTENNIAL
COMMISSION

KANSAS—THE 34TH STAR

Publication Staff

Editor-in-Chief: Nyle H. Miller
Co-editors: Edgar Langsdorf, Robert W. Richmond, Joseph W. Snell, Thomas A. Witty, Eugene D. Decker
Staff Photography: Earl F. Kintner
Special Photography: Donald P. Richards, Topeka, and Patricia D. Duncan, Lake Quivira
Art and Layout: Donald Shurtz, Patterson Advertising Agency, Topeka
Copy Typist: Mrs. Patricia P. Anderson

109
108
107
106
105
104
103 Longitude
44
43
40
39
38
37
36
31
30
28
27
26
BIG HORN MOUNTS
CROW INDIANS
BLACK HILLS
ATTACHED to DACOTAH
Rock Independence
SOUTH PASS
Sweet Water R.
Table Hills
Pilot Butte
Laramie Peak
LARAMIE PLAINS
Ft. Laramie
North Fork of Platte River
Scotts Bluff
Chimney Rock
Ancient Ruins
Bridgers Pass
Cheyenne Pass
OGALALA DACOTA
Lodge Pole Cr.
NORTH PARK
LARIMER
Remarkable Rocks
White Butte
SUMMIT
WELD
Fremonts Butte
Longs Peak
BOULDER
MIDDLE PARK
DENVER CITY
Auraria
GOLD REGION
ARAPAHOE
Breckinridge
Jefferson
DOUGLAS
Blue River
Grand R.
SOUTH PARK
COLORADO
Colorado City
Pikes Peak
EL PASO
INDIANS
Reservation of the Cheyennes and Arapaches
Canon City
Fountain City
PUEBLO
FREMONT
Cochetope Pass
Pueblo
Bents Ft.
Trading Post
LA PLATA MOUNTAINS
COSTILLA
CONEJOS
Ft. Garland
Spanish Peaks
HUERFANO
Purgatory River
NEW MEXICO
El Alto del Utah
Ojo de S. José
Abiquiu Peak
Ranchitos
Taos
Trampas
Ft. Union
SANTA FE
ROCKY MOUNTAINS
Drawn and Engraved by W. H. Gamble, Philad.a